# HIS favor

*It's Not About Obtaining Favor...*
*It's About Recognizing You Already Have It.*

*by*

Stephanie D. Moore

Published by
*Moore Marketing and Communications*
Oklahoma City, Oklahoma
www.StephanieDMoore.com

Bulk copies or group sales of this book are available by contacting moore@stephaniedmoore.com or by calling (405) 248-7038.

FIRST EDITION PRINTED NOVEMBER 2015
Printed in USA

*Moore, Stephanie D.*
In HIS Favor: 31 Day Devotional
First Edition.

Library of Congress Control Number: 2015919189
1. Jesus  2. Favor  3. Devotional  4. Spirituality  5. Religion  6. Christianity 7. God

Issued also as an ebook.

ISBN: 978-0-9962040-9-5

# In HIS Favor
*Devotionals*

*"Glory to God in the highest heaven,*
*and on earth peace to those on whom his favor rests."*
*Luke 2:14*

# HIS favor

## Purpose

The purpose of this publication is to share key points in my life in which I never, while experiencing them, considered or imagined that I was in the favor of God. As I look back on those days, I realize God was not only in each situation, he was blessing me in every experience... even when they were tear-filled and embarrassingly humbling.

This book is meant to bless the reader by allowing each day to become a celebration. As we suffer unexpected loss, rejection, humiliation and heartbreak, we still have value we can bring and ways to love the life we are living. Whether we cherish our health, family, education, opportunities or successes, there is always a reason to praise the Lord.

Before you start considering the laundry list of problems you may be facing, know—we are all facing serious issues that seem insurmountable and possibly unbearable. However, there is one person we can trust to carry the burdens we hold, if we dare.

I hope that as I learned to trust God, you will as well.
It has been the best choice I ever made in my life.
I am forever, in His Favor.

# In the Midst of Gratitude

*"And whatever you do in word or deed, do all in the name of the Lord Jesus,*
*giving thanks to God and the Father by him."*
*Colossians 3:17*

## In Context

Colossians 3 bears a heavy weight of instruction. First, it shares
with us the glorious and unmistakable reasons we have for following
Christ. It states that since we have been saved by the grace of Christ
Jesus, who now sits beside the Father on his right side, we should
think as saints and forget what the earth says is good (money, sex
and power which pour into pride and lead to false worship) When
the Lord elected to offer His perfect gift of salvation, we inherited
the riches and glory that come with it. For Christ is all and is in all.
Therefore we should give thanks to God, singing His praises and
teaching others of His goodness by way of action or word.

## THE POWER OF THANK YOU

I once worked tirelessly to put together a program for women. It
cost me all of what I had to make it happen. But of the ten women
invited, only a few showed up with consistency. Some never showed
or called. Thousands of dollars in the hole, I began to lose hope. I
was tired, down to my last monies and upset that the women didn't
appreciate what was offered. I would have loved for someone to
simply gift me some of what we provided them.

We offered the ladies a week of pampering: hair styles, manicures, pedicures, massages and gift baskets. We also offered a variety of classes, a dinner with keynote speaker and a photo shoot. During the week, on the way to one of the classes I began to cry as I spoke with the instructor for that evening's class. We were both en route, she traveling from a great distance and I running on my last leg of energy. I confessed to her I didn't think many of the ladies would come. She insisted that those who chose to receive the blessing are those the gift is for. We agreed that I provided the provisions as instructed by God, but only those that actually wanted the blessing would partake. I couldn't own or feel responsible or hurt for those that denied it. I imagine God feels the same with his unwavering gift of salvation. Why should my gift be any different?

One of the ladies, posted every day online how amazing the classes were and how they were impacting her life. She shared how she knew this was in fact a gift from God and each day she shared how it made her feel. Those words of encouragement and gratitude lifted me higher and encouraged me to keep going.

While God does not need our thanks, he certainly deserves it. Consider the last time you helped someone and they DIDN'T say thank you.

> *"But thou art holy, O thou that inhabitest the praises of Israel."*
> Psalm 22:3

**In Context**
This scripture lies in a body of text, where David is crying out for peace in a situation that has caused him great distress. Every verse surrounding (above and beneath) speaks of crying out to God in the midst of his storm. David clearly understood his relationship with God and was described as a man after God's own heart. His relationship was so well-rooted in God that even in his trouble he knew praise could bring him out.

**Final Notes**
When we acknowledge all the gifts, relationships, opportunities and mercy/grace God has sanctioned in our lives, we can't help but offer

Him a mighty and loud praise. Our gratitude and attitude determine our altitude. The higher we are in Him, the more we reverence him with our actions and our words with a pure heart that is abundant in praise and worship. In Psalm 67, one such prayer is lifted. It is a song of praise to God.

---

### Prayer

Father, we humbly come before you in reverence. We give you all of the glory, honor and the praise. We thank you for this day in our lives —a time when we can reflect on your goodness and mercy. A time when we can exemplify our thank you with our thoughts and our actions. We shout HALLELUJAH! We give you all the praise! Please direct our paths and make them straight. Please help us to make choices that are pleasing in your sight. Help us to be all that you created us to be. Lord, please keep your angels encamped around us and our loved ones in protection.

*In Jesus Name, Amen.*

---

# While We Wait

*"For the revelation awaits an appointed time; it speaks of the end and will not prove false. Though it linger, wait for it, it will certainly come and will not delay."*
*Habakkuk 2:3*

## In Context

Habakkuk is concerned about the evil that rules around him. He turns to God in question, asking for guidance and a report of what is truly happening to the righteous people in his land. God reassures him that a time will come when the tables will turn and to trust in HIS truth because it will come sooner than later.

## WAITING ON GOD TO DELIVER

When I was pregnant with my oldest daughter, I was so impatient! From the very beginning a lot of my eating and sleeping habits began to change. Suddenly, my sense of smell was much sharper and my appetite grew exponentially. I craved weird and crazy things like Sonic Drive-In Fried Chicken Sandwiches with gravy and Braum's Ice Cream. Most of all, my morning sickness never passed! Yes, I endured nine months of morning sickness. Not to mention the other crazy body changes I went through carrying a child.

So here I was, 19 and pregnant. I wasn't married and I quickly went from living with my boyfriend to moving back in with my mother. We were still a couple, we just thought it would be better if I stayed with mom.

My belly got bigger and I waited. I heard her little heartbeat and I waited. I saw her figure on the sonogram… and I waited. We got engaged and I waited some more.

Finally it was almost time to give birth! In an ideal world, my daughter would have been born sometime between Christmas and New Year's. BUT, my doctor was going on vacation. So he gave me a choice, I could wait or be induced. "NO MORE WAITING!" I thought loudly. "Let's induce," I quickly pronounced. We selected her birth date for two weeks from that day (December 28th). In the interim, I was so tired of waiting on the baby, I asked my mom to drop me off at Wal-mart, so I could 'walk-her-out". Of course, that didn't work.

Finally, the day came for me to be induced. It was one of the most peaceful days of my life! They broke my water promptly at 6 am. I was in labor for 13 hours. Then she arrived. She was beautiful with a head full of hair and bright engaging eyes.

On February 10th, the following year, my husband and I were married. They were both well worth the wait!

*"Thou shalt be over my house, and according unto thy word shall all my people be ruled: only in the throne will I be greater than thou. And Pharaoh said unto Joseph, See, I have set thee over all the land of Egypt." Genesis 41:40-41*

## In Context
These scriptures lie in a body of text, describing the rise of Joseph, the son of Israel. As a young man, Joseph was provided visions in dreams that he would one day be above all in his household. After many hard years of slavery, accusations, abandonment and imprisonment – Joseph is finally free! Not only is he free, he is made ruler over a nation of people, second in command to Pharaoh himself.

## Final Notes
Times when we are willing to wait patiently for God to deliver us, we are well equipped for the blessings that follow. But if we run or try to take shortcuts, we often fall on our faces in disgust. We must

open our hearts to hear God. We have to loosen our hands and let God take the reign. When we do, we go peaceably into a victorious life and our troubles last but only a moment.

---

### Prayer

Father, we bow our heads and our hearts before you in complete submission. We are open to hear your instruction and are waiting to walk along the path you create for us. We thank you Lord Jesus for your perfect sovereignty and your overwhelming grace. We are blessed to not only speak to you but to also listen and obey. Please keep your hedge of protection around us and help us to walk undeniably and unwaveringly in your way.

*In Jesus Name, Amen.*

# Trouble Don't Last Always...

*"For we do not have a High Priest who cannot sympathize with our weaknesses,
but was in all points tempted as we are, yet without sin. Let us therefore come
boldly to the throne of grace, that we may obtain mercy and find grace to help in
the time of need."*
*Hebrews 4:15-16*

## In Context

Amen, amen and amen. I love this chapter in the Bible. For one, it
directly rests upon our faith in God. How surely do we believe in
Him? This chapter reassures us that God's every promise is true and
unwavering. It directly refers to the people in the wilderness who
could not rest in God because sin kept them in a place of "trying to
fix it". However, when we learn to let go of it and hand it over to
God, he promises to extend mercy and help in our time of greatest
need.

## TROUBLE KNOCKING ON EVERY DOOR

The most impactful moment of trouble came at a time in my life
when I was lost. I was a single mom trying to make ends meet in a
foreign place with new bad habits. Never did I need more mercy,
grace and love than at that time.

I'd just started a new job in Atlanta. New to the area and culture,
everything just felt uncomfortable. My kids were beginning new
classes in new schools, my workflow was different – competitive
and demanding, my living removed my husband and inserted my
brother and sister (who lived next door to me), socially I was alone

and seeking friendship and I began to spiral downward. I started making poor choices to "help me cope" with the responsibilities and sacrifice of being single mom, my poor disposition (I had a good job with decent pay but the cost of living was high and almost unbearable) and a lack of self-confidence.

I began to make very bad decisions. I almost killed a woman running a red light after a very stressful day at work (this was one of the many car accidents I had that year). I began to party (drugs and sex) on the weekends and allowed it to drip into my weekdays. More trouble came and I asked my estranged husband to move back in… but only after I realized I was addicted to cocaine. Life was beyond my reach.

Then one day, while under duress, I cried out to God. I held the Bible firmly in my hands and I said, "Lord, if there is anything to this, I need you to show me now." That's when I began reading the Bible and God spoke to me. I was beyond ready to listen.

*In it all, even while I was still making poor choices, I heard him whisper, "… My grace is sufficient for thee: for my strength is made perfect in weakness. Most gladly, therefore will I rather glory in my infirmities, that the power of Christ may rest upon me. "*
*2 Corinthians 12:9*

## In Context
In 2 Corinthians 12, Paul breaks down and shares that he has an issue he can't seem to overcome. He admits his embarrassment behind it and shares that he has prayed for God to remove it from him… He also shares that it is something easily viewed by the masses and that his esteem suffered greatly as a result, 'pushing him to his knees'. But Jesus refused to take the handicap… in fact he countered with a simple statement. I am enough, my grace is enough… in fact, your weakness amplifies my strength.

## Final Notes
Trouble won't last always. When it surfaces, like Paul we should be driven to our knees in prayer, turning whatever it is over to God.

This is not to say that we shouldn't be praying daily, this is to say trouble should not make us run from God, or lose faith in his ability or willingness to save us. It should in fact move us to plant both feet firmly and stand our ground confessing and believing that God is already on top of it. We must begin to rest in faith when trouble tries to tell us to panic.

---

### Prayer

Lord, thank you. Thank you for your abundant love. Thank you for your unending grace. Thank you for your faithfulness. Thank you for your blessings and favor. On this day, we release our burdens and exchange them for your light and peaceful load. We exchange our worries and anxiety for your rest. We will be quick to listen and sure to obey when you tell us to move, we will be sure to follow whenever and wherever you lead. Please forgive us of our sins and help us to be more like you each day.

*In Jesus Name, Amen.*

---

# Rejoice.
# And Again I Say, Rejoice.

*"Let all those rejoice who put their trust in You; Let them ever shout for joy,*
*because You defend them; Let those also who love Your Name be joyful in You.*
*For You, O Lord, will bless the righteous; With favor You will surround him as*
*with a shield"*
*Psalm 5:11-12*

**In Context**
David is crying out to God for help. David shares his devotion and
trust of God, as well as his knowledge of God's divine sovereignty.
He notes, "The foolish shall not stand in thy sight; thou hatest
all workers of iniquity." (Psalm 5:5) He continues to ask God for
direction and help. He finalizes the chapter with his certainty of
God's favor to those that put their trust in Him.

## TRUST IN GOD'S ABILITY TO PROTECT YOU!

When I lived in Atlanta, I was driving home from work. I was taking
the Steve Reynolds Parkway and about to turn left on Club Dr.
(heading from Norcross to Lawrenceville). It's a double-turn lane but
traffic was backed up. I was moving to the outside turning lane, just
as someone else from the opposite side (the lane that was originally
going straight) moved into the same spot. Our cars collided. We both
pulled safely off the road as we waited for the Gwinnett County
Police Department to arrive.

Once over to the side of the road, a friend of his pulled up. He said he witnessed the entire accident. (They were both either drunk or had been drinking heavily). When the officer arrived, we both admitted fault, were given tickets and sent on our way.

Two weeks later, I get a call from the insurance company. The man was suing me and claiming the accident was all my fault. A court date had been filed and I was to testify in court. I was concerned. By this time, I'd already had 5 accidents within a year and a half in Atlanta. It had taken me a month before I could drive since my last accident.

I prayed and prayed for God to help me. I'd just turned over a new leaf in my life concerning God and my trust in Him was stronger than ever before… but I still held on to fear at times of trouble.

Then I got a call from the insurance company. They told me not to worry. They have a team of lawyers and they'd already assigned one of them to my case. That since both of us admitted guilt to the Gwinnett County Police Department, nothing would come of it. At the end of the call they noted, "If you hear from Judge Judy regarding this case, respectfully decline the opportunity to appear."

Look at God. He'd turned my tears into laughter. I was so happy. All my concern and worry was soon converted to praise and gratitude. God will always see us through our toughest issues.

Did we have our day in court? Yes. Fortunately, the officer that took our statements was able to appear and I took the stand with confidence. Even when the other attorney asked me if I realized there was a solid white line for that turning lane and what I did was illegal. I simply said, "More than likely, there is…" and I admitted my guilt. That solid line was on both sides of the lane, so it wasn't just I that was in error.

God is amazing. He will defend you against enemies that try to make you look bad or destroy you without cause. You can praise him now for the victory.

*"God has not given us the spirit of fear, but of power and love and of a sound mind."*
*2 Timothy 1:7*

## In Context
In 2 Timothy 1, Paul writes a letter to Timothy while in prison. He speaks of their past departure and his sadness. He speaks of the honesty and purity of Timothy's faith and strongly encourages him not to fear where the journey of sharing his faith may lead. That God has empowered him and endowed him with the gift to speak life and that any fear he may have regarding his ministry should be admonished despite what it looks like (especially since Paul's devotion and bold preaching landed him in prison).

## Final Notes
Praise the Lord and rejoice. For God has the victory in every situation. Even when we want to worry or stress, we have to learn to sit at his feet and rest. God is our shield and our great reward. He offers us a seat beneath the shadow of his wings and willingly exchanges our heavy burdens for his light load. We have to thank him in advance for what he is doing, even when things look bleak. We can rest knowing his favor isn't fair and that as his children it is ours to have.

---

### Prayer
Lord, we bow humbly before your throne of protection, love, favor and mercy. We thank you for hearing us when we pray, for allowing us an opportunity to speak to you. Please direct our path and make it straight. Lead us in the way we should go and protect us from our enemies. You know what we need before we can utter a single word. Meet us at our point of need and help us to overcome our troubles. We thank you for your unmatched favor. We give you all of the glory, we give you all of the praise and we honor you Lord.
*Thank you for loving us in spite of us, in the mighty and magnificent name of Jesus, Amen.*

---

# Love is the Answer

*"Though I speak with the tongues of men and of angels, but have not love, I have become sounding brass or a clanging cymbal. "*
I Corinthians 13:1

## In Context

In the Bible it says that Satan is like a roaring lion. I would venture to say sounding brass or a clanging symbol is much the same. I Corinthians 13 is a set of examples laid out by Paul that basically state, you can know how to do everything in the church and still manage to walk with a lack of love. You can speak in tongues, lead the choir, teach bible study, have faith… or perform any religious act but if you do it without love… it means nothing. It is like a sounding brass or a lion's roar. I love that in the end of the chapter, he strongly indicates that it is simply time to grow up. When we decide to allow maturity to reign, everything that seems unclear will become clear. Finally, he ends the chapter with a three-fold cord to completeness, assuring us love is the best or strongest cord.

## <u>Looking for Love in All the Wrong Places</u>

It's true. We are insatiable by nature and Lord knows, I am no different. In my mind, since I was a young child, I knew what the perfect man would be: loving, caring, respectful, a provider and handsome. One day, at the mall, I met him… my dream guy. LOL. I hear you laughing too! I was 19 and fell head over heels in love. I would do anything for him and I though he would do anything for me.

Then we showed up in the relationship. Yup, just like that newly baptized church in Corinth… the real us began to show and our relationship got "complicated". My desire for more and his desire for contentment clashed immediately. Rather than be a "stay-at-home" mom (which in hind sight may have been the best plan), I knew I needed to be working. I wanted more out of life and I knew it required hard work and ambition. No one could stop me!

Eventually, our relationship became a facsimile of what once was. Love was gone and every activity resembled a roaring lion (loud, disrupt and unsettled). Our insatiable appetites for more, our pride in family (no one could know we weren't madly in love) and our immaturity led us down a path of pain and hurt.

We were married 16 years. Yes, we did and still do love one another… but it took a lot of tough situations and hard lessons to get there. We were looking to define our love in all the wrong places and barely knew what love actually meant.

Much like God's love, true love never ends it simply begins when you choose to love.

*"The Lord has appeared of old to me, saying: 'Yes, I have loved you with an everlasting love; Therefore with lovingkindness I have drawn you.'"*
*Jeremiah 31:3*

### In Context
In Jeremiah 31, God is reassuring his promise of everlasting love to his people. He is establishing a brand new way for Israel and Judah. He promises restoration and joy. He promises to write his law within their hearts and to be their God, a true friend and loved one that is dependable and will love them for life. He says that when he mentions (I am going to say) our name, his heart bursts with longing for us. In return, everything in us cries out for Him. That is love. He is the only love that can fill an insatiable heart as His love is truly everlasting. He states his love can't be measured much like the core of the earth can't be found or the sky measured with a measuring stick. It is the promise of Zion, truly heaven on earth… a city that

will never be destroyed.

**Final Notes**

I must admit, love is not an easy way to go. Sometimes, we want to be angry and lash out. Sometimes we simply want revenge. Other times it is more convenient to be indifferent or uncaring. But, in the end, love IS the answer. Love answers to all things. It's not easy. Our demonstrated love required an innocent man be given the death penalty as he was willingly accused of all of our crimes. All of our crimes were placed on his books. He bore the debt of death to save our lives. Buying a homeless person something to drink or eat can't compare. Praying over a loved one who needs you to intercede doesn't measure up. No. No act of love we can give will ever compare to the gift of love we have received.

---

**Prayer**

My Savior, My God, My Friend and My Love. I thank you for my life. I thank you for the air I breathe and the thoughts in me. I thank you for allowing me to be a vessel of strength, courage, boldness and most importantly love. Your love saved me just in the nick of time, it was not late and it did not tarry. It was everything you promised it would be. You are faithful in your promise to love us unconditionally. You promised that we could come boldly before the throne of grace in our time of trouble and receive from your overflowing cup of knowledge and instruction, thank you. As we journey forward in our lives, embracing maturity, we look with open and clear eyes seeing lives that are not only touched by your love, but by the love you have so gracefully given for us to give. Please forgive us of our sins and help us to be more like you each day.
*In Jesus Name, Amen.*

---

# Holy, Holy, Holy

*"So Samuel said: 'Has the Lord as great delight in burnt offerings and sacrifices, as in obeying the voice of the Lord? Behold, to obey is better than sacrifice, and to heed than the fat of rams."*
I Samuel 15:22

## In Context

Saul was anointed King over Israel. As king, he had many responsibilities. The most important was to obey the Word of God as delivered to him by Samuel. In this chapter, God ordered Saul to destroy the Amalekites completely. He was to leave nothing and take nothing. Instead, he kept what he desired and didn't even kill the king of the Amalekites. He and his men went through and kept whatever seemed desirable. So, as Samuel the prophet approached, Saul boldly calls out, "God's Blessings on you! I accomplished God's plan to the letter!" Which only added insult to injury because it further indicated that he knew he did what he wanted and not what God instructed. Instead he allowed the people to direct Him and his decisions. God's immediate response was regret. "I'm sorry I ever made Saul king. He's turned his back on me. He refused to do what I tell him."

## OBEDIENCE **NOT** COMFORT

To obey is love. We know when we tell our kids to clean their room or do a chore… we expect, even demand they do it without question. When they question us or choose to do it their way instead of the way we instruct we are beyond upset. Why? Because there is a reason we have asked them to perform in a certain way. When we see their effort is real and sincere (even if they miss the mark) we are proud of them.

When I was transitioning from a drug addict to a Christian… my walk was not easy. I fell and bumped my head more times than I would care to share. Sometimes my efforts were sincere, other times I just gave in to my personal desire and did what I thought I wanted.

I thank God for grace because it is due to his unending grace that I am still here. But, that grace didn't change the consequences of my choices. No, the punishment stayed the same and the forgiveness came but not without due shame. I had to walk with my head hanging low and wear this badge labeled drug addict before my friends and family for years. Some of them still affix that label and there is nothing I can do about what they think.

It wasn't until I truly trusted God to do it for me and truly desire His will above my own that victory over my demons came. I just couldn't do it on my own. I need his Holy Spirit, His Word and His love to make it.

*"If you love Me, keep My commandments. He who has My commandments and keeps them, it is he who loves Me. And he who loves Me will be loved by My Father, and I will love him and manifest Myself to him."*
*John 14:15, 21*

## In Context
Let not your heart be troubled… This is a chapter I truly love. In this chapter, Jesus shares with his disciples that his time with them is coming to an end and beginning in a different way. It is truly a chapter I love because in a lot of ways it breaks down the trilogy in realistic terms. One of the disciples says, "Show us the Father and then we will be content." Content. Not happy, not overjoyed, not grateful… content. Jesus then assures him that he has already in fact seen the Father, in Him. That not only has he seen the Father, but he will also receive the Holy Spirit. God has given us the gift of his presence in every way possible. He promises further within the chapter that if they only abide in him, being obedient (which is love)

he will continue to make himself visible and plain to them. He then shares that a loveless world is a sightless world. Obedience is love.

**Final Notes**
Obedience is uncomfortable at times because it requires us to rewire the way we think and approach a situation. If you want to be healed you have to pick up your mat and walk. You can't blame the world around you for your lack of obedience or lack of love toward God. It is always a choice we must make within ourselves. Once we have made the choice to truly obey God our true love for him is evident. Not only will God begin to honor us, but others will as well because they will easily see him in and operating through us.

---

### Prayer

Lord, we come humbly before your throne of mercy, love and grace with hearts filled with gratitude and reverence. Lord, please direct our path and make it straight. Help us to remember your word and your will when we make decisions. If there is a thought process we are embracing that is out of alignment with your will help us to fully understand what we must to realign our thoughts with yours. For we know our ways are not your ways and that our thoughts are not your thoughts… that your thoughts are higher than ours. We give you all of the honor, all of the glory, all of the praise.
*Help us to obey your word, in the name of Jesus we pray. Amen.*

# Forgiveness. Mercy. Grace.

*"Many sorrows shall be to the wicked: but he that trusteth in the Lord, mercy shall compass him about."*
*Psalm 32:10*

## In Context

Psalm 32 speaks of having a confident confession of sin to God. David says that when he tried to keep his sins in, moving along as though nothing had occurred it would eat away at his soul (new wine in an old wineskin). He further asserts how blessed we are to be able to take our sins to God and be forgiven. That we can trust God to forgive us and guide us further along the way. The way I read the King James Version, (as we are all allowed our own interpretation) it sounds like God's response to David in the latter half confirms what David has said while asserting the unfortunate decision to wallow in sin and have to be forced into asking for forgiveness with painful situations. Instead, we should learn to trust God with our whole being and choices (even when we make horrible decisions) and celebrate the fact that he gives us VIP Access to the throne.

## STUMBLING DOWN A HILL OF POOR DECISION

Imagine a young man whose mother has instructed him to tie his shoes. She repeatedly makes the statement but the boy ignores her instructions. As they journey down the hill, a rabbit hops across his path, suddenly and unexpectedly. He trips over his lose shoe strings and begins to tumble down the hill. As he falls, his head hits a rock and he is knocked unconscious. His mother calls for help and his is soon taken to the hospital. As he awakes, he sees his mother's beautiful face looking down at him with eyes that are filled with concern. She doesn't ask him a thing, she doesn't accuse him or say, "I told you so". She just lovingly looks at him and gently places her hand on his face. Tears well up in his eyes as he apologizes to her repeatedly. The first thing he remembered as he looked up at his mother was her telling him to tie his shoes. This is how God works in our lives. He knows that sometimes it takes a mighty and tough fall for us to "get it". But, he truly desires for us to just "get it" the first time.

While living in Atlanta, I had several car accidents. After a tough day at work, I was clearly distracted driving home. A 15-minute drive easily took an hour due to traffic. As I was traveling between stoplights, I almost ran one. In my head, I heard very clearly, "Slow down and pay attention or you will be in an accident." It was as clear as a bell and trust me when I say, I remember being at that stoplight with my bangs sticking straight up (which is what I do when I am stressed, I run my fingers through my hair and stick it straight up in the air – not sure when that started but it is definitely a sign that I am stressed). As I got to the next light, I picked up my cellphone to call my cousins who were at my house waiting for me. When I looked up, the light was yellow and about to turn red. I decided to run the light. As I begin to go through the light, I see a woman in a car emerge from behind a bush (which was at the opposing stoplight blocking any cars that may be at the light). I panicked. I knew in my heart, I was going to hit this woman and hard. I was afraid I might kill her. I instantly raised my hands to pray. I prayed, "Lord, please don't let me kill this woman." CRASH. I t-boned her vehicle and hit the tail end of her driver's seat and backseat. She was alive but her back was badly injured.

When the officer asked me what happened, I told him I ran the red light. On the back of my insurance card, it clearly stated to never admit guilt. I didn't care, it was the truth and I was just glad I didn't kill her.

I wish I'd paid attention when God warned me, but I didn't. It took hindsight for me to see that he tried to save me from the trouble…

tried to warn me, but I wasn't listening. Instead, I had to learn the lesson the hard way and ask for forgiveness.

*"If we confess our sins, He is faithful and just to forgive us our sins and to cleanse us from all unrighteousness."*
I John 1:9

## In Context

I John 1 is a celebration and culmination of the life of Jesus. It doesn't break down act by act but more explains the fulfillment of purpose. One, to celebrate that our Savior is real, died on the cross for us, is alive and loves us. Two, to ensure us that if we claim to live in Him and do not mirror him, we are not truly living the life we claim. Three, if we pretend that we are perfect, we are not only liars, we don't understand God. As believers in Jesus, we can have every intent on walking in righteousness (self-created) and mess up royally. We can be committed to be obedient and still fail. This is who we are… people. God surely doesn't expect us to be perfect. In fact, he knows there is no possible way for us to be perfect because it's not in our DNA. What we can do and are expected to do is bring those concerns and mistakes to God and allow Him to walk us through and help us get to the road of righteousness.

## Final Notes

We live in a world full of people carrying baggage they were never intended to carry. Critical self-examination allows their past decisions to echo like a broken record that plays over and over in their heads. Sometimes, we carry things we never confess to God because we are too afraid to even confess that it was wrong or a poor decision to ourselves which can lead us into self-destruction or a closed mind that is focused only on self. God sent his son Jesus as a form of himself so that we didn't have to suffer alone. So we didn't have to perform outright open sacrifices to try and rectify our sins (but we still see people doing that… trying to find a way to make it right… we do that). God doesn't want us to try and "figure it out". Instead, he offered a solution and gift to not only help us forgive ourselves, but to operate in forgiveness of others… to extend mercy as we have received it and to fully appreciate the gift of grace.

## Prayer

Thank you Jesus for your forgiveness, mercy and grace. It's a gift we could not earn or deserve but one you have granted to us willingly. Lord, please help us to be brave enough to admit our faults to you, to entrust our failures to your everlasting perfection and to trust you in with our deepest inner turmoil. While we are not perfect, we pray that you will help us to be more like you each day. Help us to listen when you speak and to take heed to your warnings. Help us to live a life that is reflective of you. Teach us and help us to bless others that may be suffering from critical self-examination, self-destruction and/or selfishness. If that person is us, we ask that you help us to see and hear you clearly.

*We love and honor you in the name of Jesus we pray, Amen.*

## DAY 8

# *Growing, Building and Success*

*"And whatsoever ye do, do it heartily, as to the Lord, and not unto men; Knowing that of the Lord ye shall receive the reward of inheritance: for ye serve the Lord Christ. But he that doeth wrong shall receive for the wrong which he hath done: and there is no respect of persons."*
*Colossians 3:23-25*

### In Context

Seeing things from God's perspective isn't easy or our first course of action. But in Colossians 3, Paul breaks it down. He explains that our "real life" which is life in Christ is a completely different life than the one we've lived or are well-acquainted with. The life we know and remember was led by emotion and desire which angers God. The gift of an emerged life is kindness, humility, purity, quiet strength and self-control.

### WHEN I LOOK BACK

This title is in present tense for a reason. For some reason, just like Lot's wife, I have a tendency to look back. It often starts with a glance, transitions into a tiptoe and next thing you know I am strutting in my ignorance. It's real. I can't lie. So, when I began this Bible study, I was convicted in my heart. God knows how to get me right where I need to be.

I've never had a problem with hard work. Anything that keeps my mind off of me (truth) helps me to have peace and know I am doing a good thing. So, I stay busy with whatever I can.

However, in my hard work, in my busyness, I have to have

interactions with others. It is in those communications and interactions I am usually drawn one of three ways, intense pleasure, indifference or great pain. What can I say, I am a full on passionate person and often, this is led by my emotions and/or my perception of your opinion.

Validation from others keeps us locked in a prison. I've always relished in open, apparent validation. If you can communicate (in any way) to me that I am doing a good job and that you appreciate my presence in your life, you will get more of the same. It really doesn't have to be in public or before men, it just needs to be communicated in word or deed.

So, naturally, when I received Christ as my Savior I worked extra hard to receive his validation. But he showed me, that too much of that is vanity and not so much for his glory as it was my own. He furthered showed me that he sees our true motives by looking into our hearts… so that was always my measure, what is my heart saying?

I noticed that when I felt vulnerable or judged, I would often revert back to my old ways. I would mask my pain with bad behavior. I would change my persona to reflect a person that couldn't be hurt, that couldn't feel pain and that wouldn't accept mess from anyone. But inside, I would be dying, even crying for help. The walls of my prison of validation would close in on me.

I learned that a life of balance and staying in constant communication, worship and learning from God is the only way a person can survive. That trusting Him and His ways is the only way to go. Whenever we try to take our own path, or "follow the leader" (whomever that may be), we end up in a bad place.

God convicts and swiftly divides my thoughts and actions with His Word and His ways. He won't allow me to travel too far down that road before he intercedes.

I hate when I have to get that butt whooping from God! It is not fun, in fact it is often gut-wrenching, embarrassing, seemingly overwhelming and… needed. I thank God that he is the best father a girl could have. When I work to please an audience of one (absence of vanity and personal glory) I am in his perfect will and the doors of opportunity, blessings and increase arrive.

*"This Book of the Law shall not depart from your mouth, but you shall meditate in it day and night, that you may observe to do according to all that is written in it. For then you will make your way prosperous, and then you will have good success."*
*Joshua 1:8*

## In Context

Joshua was to have a right now faith. He was not permitted to wait, or think about it or be afraid. He was to move forward in courageous confidence that God was with him. Not only was he to move forward, he was to do exactly as God instructed him to do... nothing more, nothing less. The soldiers within the camp (who'd already received their possessions) had to cross over the Jordan River in BATTLE formation while leading and helping their brothers until God gave THEIR BROTHERS rest. Then and only then, would they be free to return to their God given possessions. The soldiers responded with confident obedience and promised to KILL whomever chose NOT to OBEY. Finally, they encouraged Joshua to be strong and courageous.

## Final Notes

We can self-destruct if we look to man and consider their opinion over God. We can imprison ourselves in validation and outward glory. But, if we are careful to measure our hearts and remain in the will of God, we will see success. We have to stay grounded in His Word and stay in His presence. When we do, God will order our steps and tell us which way to go. He may reveal our destination (like he did with Joshua) or he may only reveal our next step. Whatever he instructs we have to be willing to move with confidence. We may have to fight a couple of battles, but in our quiet strength and humble obedience, we will survive and thrive.

## Prayer

What a mighty God we serve. Lord, you have the ability to see within us and see our hearts. You can speak to us in ways that not only direct us, but can correct us with love and gentleness. We thank you for your everlasting arm of protection. We thank you for not sparing the rod... for without it, we could not recognize our faults. We thank you for the opportunity to pray and we honor your perfect way. Lord, as we embark on the journey you have set before us, help us to be courageously confident. Help us not to waiver from your direction. Help us to be ready and prepared for the battle that is before us and help us to stay united as one unit serving under God.

*In the mighty and magnificent name of Jesus we pray, Amen.*

# Praise Him!

*"Oh magnify the Lord with me, and Let us exalt his name together."*
*Psalm 34:3*

## In Context

I will bless the Lord at all times. This is the premise of Psalm 34. This response is drawn from the heart and soul as David reflects on all that God has done for him. Worship was an integral part of David's life. Within the chapter, he shares the goodness of God, his protection and the fact that he will listen to your prayers when you call.

## GIVING GOD THE GLORY!

There have been so many situations in my life that warrant giving God the glory but one of the more prevalent episodes was when I was just beginning my career. I worked 3 jobs and attended school during the day. I worked afternoon to evening at a local TV station. I worked late evening to 7 am overnight at a rental car reservation center. I attended class from 8 am – 3 pm. I worked part-time in the marketing department at the school from 3 to 5 pm. I didn't work every job every day but I worked at least 2 jobs every day. I was tired, but I refused to give up hopes in my dreams. There were days when my limbs would go to sleep because I couldn't. There were times I nearly got fired from that overnight job because I would accidentally fall asleep on the phone. Nonetheless, I made it.

One day, while in the marketing department, the marketing director

approached me. She told me they had an open position as the
graphic design coordinator and I should apply.

I knew the position was open, but I honestly never thought I'd
be considered. Up until that time, I worked primarily in video
animation. I would create opens for our videos and created on-air
graphics for the news station. She strongly encouraged me to apply.
So, I did.

During the interview, they asked several questions about how I
would respond to specific situations… I answered as candidly as
possible (I really didn't think I would get the job and everyone in the
department I considered a close friend). I even went so far as to tell
them what I thought they should have asked me and what a person
in that position should really be doing. LOL.

Later that week, the marketing director approached me again with a
giant smile on her face. She said, "Stephanie, you interviewed very
well." I smiled and said, "OK", with a 'I'm tired and I have a lot of
work to do so can you get to the point face.' She looked at me again
and said, "Really good". LOL. I didn't get it… I was too tired to
even care!

Needless to say, I got the job and it was my first career focused job.
I was ecstatic, 9 am – 5 pm with benefits and career development
travel. It was amazing.

I was tired and worn out but I refused to quit. I wouldn't give up. I
was determined to make my dreams come true. I couldn't help but
give God all the glory!

*"It is a good thing to give thanks unto the Lord, and to sing praises unto thy*
*name, O most High: To shew forth thy lovingkindness in the morning and thy*
*faithfulness every night."*
*Psalm 92: 1-2*

**In Context**
Originally written as a song to God and sung on the Sabbath, David sings of a faithful and loving God. A Lord who avenges the hurts enemies may inflict and protects his people. He totes of the great works of the Lord and his thoughts. He finishes with those that are planted in the Lord shall flourish in the courts of God.

**Final Notes**
No matter how hard we are working or how little our acknowledgment is, we know that God sees and knows all. He is going to bless us if we just hold on and keep the faith.

---

### Prayer

Lord, we thank you. We thank you and praise you because there is no man like you. There is no one that we can compare to you. You are our father, our confidant, our protector, our director, our provider and our savior. You willingly sacrificed your all to save our all. We can't thank or honor you enough. Nothing we do or say can adequately communicate your wonderful works, thoughts or plans for our lives. Help us to be more like you, loving our neighbors as we love ourselves. Help us to intercede on behalf of those in leadership. Help us to lift up and love our fellow man. Lord, forgive us when we fall short or refuse to obey.
*We love you and thank you in the mighty and merciful name of Jesus, Amen.*

# The Blessed Relationship

*"You are my friends, if you do whatsoever I command you. No longer do I call you servants, for a servant does not know what his master is doing; but I have called you friends, for all things that I heard from My Father I have made known to you. You did not choose Me, I chose you and appointed you that you should go and bear fruit, and that your fruit should remain, that whatever you ask the Father in My name He may give you."*
John 15:14-16

## In Context

Jesus shares critical information with his disciples prior to his departure. He has elected each one to serve in his ministry and shared knowledge and prophecy of things to come. In this chapter, he insists they recognize that as long as they stay connected to him and obedient (which is love – friends give reciprocal love) they will continue to bear fruit and will receive the gift of the Holy Spirit to comfort them in times of need. He also shares that even though they don't deserve it they will be persecuted just as he has and soon will be. Finally, he shares that they will bear witness and testify, just as he has, because they have been with him since the beginning.

## IN THE BEGINNING

God, Jesus and Holy Spirit. I love any scripture that reflects the trinity in action. You can see this in Genesis as they discuss the Tower of Babel and when they go and visit Abraham and Sarah before the fall of Gomorrah. It reflects the relationship God had with Abraham. The friendship that existed.

We see it so many times in the Bible… God and Enoch, God and Moses, God and Noah, God and Abraham, God and Rahab, God and Esther, God and David, God and Joseph. Now we see Jesus and Mary Magdalene, Jesus and Zacchaeus, Jesus and the Woman with the Issue of Blood, Jesus and the Woman at the Well, Jesus and Peter, Jesus and Nicodemus. Finally, we see the Holy Spirit and Paul, the Holy Spirit and Stephen, the Holy Spirit and Us.

In the beginning of my new found love for Christ and after I was baptized, on Valentine's Day, my husband looked at me midday and asked what I wanted for the holiday. I have to admit I was angry that he waited so long to even acknowledge it was Valentine's Day and then to nonchalantly ask the question sent me into a different dimension. I shrugged and stayed silently angry. He immediately left the house and returned within 10 minutes. He purchase this little ugly monkey with a heart in his hand and a pair of nice headphones.

I'd just began writing music (not real music – Stephanie's this is what I think a song is… music) and he was supportive. Not soon after, he moved out during what was our final separation right before divorce.

I kept that little monkey but when I looked at it, all I saw was a moment of anger in my life. Then I watched a movie that changed my perspective, the new version of King Kong. It was during a time when many storms were raging in my life… the desire to do things I had no business doing, loss of friends due to lifestyle changes (choosing Christ over partying) and financial hardship.

I watched as King Kong fell in love with this woman that was offered up to him as a sacrifice. She was afraid of his great stature and obvious power but was able to recognize his sweet and caring disposition toward her. Many of the dangerous animals (dinosaurs and what not) wanted to eat her and as King Kong protected her, he would throw her from hand to hand and foot to foot keeping her out of harm's way. She was being tossed and every time it looked like one of those animals was going to eat her or hurt her, just in the nick of time, he would remove her from danger.

All the while, her friends were trying to rescue her from this strange beast they couldn't understand, feared and didn't know. It was ironic because it was a picture of my life unfolding before my eyes. Danger was at every turn, but God interceded just in time before I was destroyed… my old friends were trying to pull from the church saying I was doing too much and going too deep but that came from fear and a lack of understanding.

I fell madly in love with that little ugly monkey my ex-husband purchased… it began to look so beautiful to me. Somewhere I found a little baby monkey and it fit perfectly in the big monkey's arm that held the heart. I would hug that monkey many nights when storms arose and my pillowcase was stained with tears. I knew this doll didn't represent God, but it was tangible, it was mine and it helped in a weird way for me to visibly feel God's presence.

There were days when the little monkey had fallen out of the big monkey's arms and I would say, "Yup, that is exactly where I am… operating out of your will." It was funny because although it was simply symbolic in nature, it was very comforting.

That monkey represented the relationship God had with me… and that I had with him. That I was his child, small and trusting, wrapped in his love. It is a blessed relationship.

*"Show Your marvelous lovingkindness by Your right hand, O You who save those who trust in You. From those who rise up against them. Keep me as the apple of Your eye; Hide me under the shadow of Your wings, From the wicked who oppress me, From my deadly enemies who surround me."*
*Psalm 17: 7-9*

## In Context

David knew his relationship with God was blessed. He understood early on in life as he was tending sheep that God was with him everywhere he went. Psalm 17 is a prayer of safety. David stood before God with open and honest dialogue, begging God to look at his circumstance and save him from his enemies. He vowed that he wasn't trying to win by the world's standards, but trying to win by God's standard and the way God instructed him to go.

**Final Notes**

Like many of the relationships God had with people noted in the Bible, we can look back at our relationship with the Lord. When he saves us from our many enemies, including the one that looks back at us in the mirror each morning. God is such a good friend that not only did he ordain us for good works, he sent his Son to save us and his Holy Spirit to keep us… who can asked for a more blessed relationship?

Side note: As I used the headphones my ex-husband bought, I wrote and recorded "To Sir with Love" a poem and song dedicated to my love for God… what initially angered me proved to be a pair of the most precious gifts sent directly from God through my ex-husband… how ironic. Often, we judge unjustly and far too soon.

---

### Prayer

Heavenly Father, to say we love you isn't enough. To thank you for this or for that alone, will not suffice. We surrender our lives to you in true worship. We promise to testify and share as instructed. Help us to bear fruit and reflect our love for you as you have freely given it to us. Help us to become perfect conduits of your love, mercy and grace. Cleanse us of iniquity and self-gratification that is displeasing in you sight. Direct us and protect us Lord as we travel along this journey. Help us to hear your voice clearly in a world that screams distraction after distraction.
*In Jesus name we pray, Amen.*

---

# Seed & Harvest

*"In the morning sow your seed, and at evening withhold not your hand, for you do not know which will prosper, this or that, or whether both alike will be good."*
*Ecclesiastes 11:6*

## In Context

Solomon, touted the wisest man to ever live, gives wonderful advice about charity and hard work. He advises that you give and give because it will always yield a great return and because we never know when our last day will arrive. He also insists that we work hard and tirelessly, being diligent to complete the work that is set before us. Don't watch and look to see what everyone else is doing, do what God has called YOU to do.

## WHEN GOD CALLED ME TO GIVE

I remember the day distinctly. It was December of 2013, about a week before Christmas. I was expressing my gratitude to God for bringing me a mighty long way and reflecting on how far I'd come. In that moment of unfiltered, private worship I felt an urge in my spirit. I knew the core of all of my personal problems began and corralled around low self-esteem.

Point blank, I cared more about what others thought and wore their opinions on my person like clothing. I didn't give my opinion of self any value.

My job, my marriage, my children and my possessions determined my self-worth. I grew up poor watching my mom take care of us by herself. She worked two jobs. Not only did I miss her affirmations (she was too tired to really give them) but I also missed the affirmations only a father could give his daughter. The only affirmations I had were presented in the admiration of others… and I worked hard to get them.

This mental thought process took me down a road of self-destruction. It wasn't until I began to have a relationship with God that I learned my true value and began to really define my self-worth. That's when my personal development, career and business began to flourish.

So, on that evening in December after dinner, I heard God whisper, "You aren't the only one. There are others that hurt just as much as you did." So that night, I designed a logo for "Kiss Your Self-Esteem". I wrote the following on Facebook:

So. I have no idea where God is going with this, but I do know it is going to launch on Valentine's Day. KYSE (pronounced kissy) stands for Kiss Your Self Esteem. The program is meant to encourage former drug addicts, rape victims, unwed mothers or women with low self-esteem to start loving themselves.

I know this is the first step in becoming happy - loving who you are, where you are, regardless of your circumstance or past.

I believe it all begins with someone else showing you how valuable you are. This year on Valentine's Day I am going to make a couple women feel the true gift of love… If you know a special woman in the Oklahoma City area that could use this special day of pampering, please inbox me.

If you would like to donate time, a special gift or offer prayer, they are all welcomed.

It was the very first seed of substantial size and required substantial faith for me to give. It cost so much for me (a single parent with two jobs just like my mom) in time and money. I offered 10 women a week of pampering and daily devotions. I paid for hairstyles, mani-pedis, facials and one hour massages. Finally, we held a catered dinner with a professional photographer and fabulous keynote address given by Lisa Miller Baldwin. It was expensive (for me).

To make matters worse, during the last week, I had interviews and donations coming from all over the Nation… but God was dealing with me and my unaddressed mess. All of these emotions about being molested swam in that week. Memories I buried, conversations with adults after… the whole nine. I was a mess… and the money for everything I planned had not come in. My faith was tested like never before. I cried a river of tears that week. I was a hot mess!

BUT GOD! He made it all come together and quite successfully. From the outside looking in, you would never know all that I went through.

When I made it through that first event, I knew I could do more. This birthed 'She's a BOSSE' and 'Grindaholix', both are youth programs for teens and created in 2014.

But, by September of 2014, I was laid off. I cried, "Lord, why in the world? I keep doing what you tell me to but bad stuff keeps happening!" How many of us have been here?

Now, my once part-time business is full time. I have authored two books and can easily see four more. I have been hired as a campaign manager for a prominent business person in our area. I cannot complain.

Yes, I work hard. I have to. I don't have much of a choice… but with God at the helm, I will continue to do so and continue to give as he allows. He has opened doors no man can shut. I have planted seed and I am reaping a harvest… Praise the Lord!

*"Except the LORD build the house, they labour in vain that build it: except the LORD keep the city, the watchmen waketh but in vain."*
*Psalm 127:1*

## In Context

Unless God is doing it, we are wasting our time. No amount of effort or feigned protection will be able to withstand the enemy's trials without keeping God first. In Psalm 127, God explains that his children are like arrows. ARROWS! Arrows in the hand of a MIGHTY man. He further explains that they will not be ashamed!

## Final Notes

What a mighty God we serve. His ways and his instructions may not make perfect sense to us but when we are obedient, we will see his plan to fruition. Planting seed is difficult, a seed must be watered and nurtured before it becomes a flourishing plant. There is a lot of work that happens underground before we even begin to see something sprout.

---

### Prayer

Lord, Jesus, you know us by name. You know our situations and you know our destination. Help us to do your will even when it doesn't make sense. Help us to trust you in spite of what our bank accounts or situations try to convince us is happening. Help us to align our action with your direction. Forgive us for all of our sins.
*In Jesus name we pray, Amen.*

---

# *Protection*

*"The eyes of the Lord run to and fro throughout the whole earth, to show
Himself strong on behalf of those whose heart is loyal to Him."*
*2 Chronicles 16:9a*

## In Context
Asa was the King of Judah. He'd developed an outstanding
relationship with God by being obedient and seeking God's guidance
in all things. In Asa's reign, Judah experienced peace and rest from
their enemies because they trusted God and removed as many areas
of false worship as possible. Unfortunately, after 36 years in office,
Asa no longer went to God before making decisions. This cost him a
serious battle and later on, yet consequently, his life.

## TRANSITIONING AND SAFE
I was a drug addict. I used cocaine on a regular basis for about
2 years. Along the way, I lost friend after friend and family soon
abandoned me as well. I was alone and exactly where God wanted me
to be.

I began reading the Bible and praying. I began to worship God as I
understood worship to be. I hadn't completely walked away from my
sinful ways, as many might say, 'I had one foot in and one foot out'.

I was dropping off an offering equivalent to the amount I spent on
drugs each week to any church I could find along the way. Most of
the time, I could slip the money under the door when I knew no one

was there. I didn't want to talk to anyone, I just wanted God to know, the drugs weren't more important to me than he was.

I would often buy drugs from different dealers because I didn't want any one dealer to know how much or how often I was using… it was shameful.

The funny part about it all is that I would have lengthy conversations with these men about Jesus every time I went to buy. One of them, facing a trial soon began to tell me how his mother would be so proud to know he was talking about Jesus. It was ironic, the situation, but nonetheless, very true.

Well, one day I was going to buy from a new dealer. I'd bought from him a couple times before. He stood 6' 5" and probably weighed 270 lbs. His house was way out in the country where you couldn't get any reception and surrounded by pit bulls. I am deathly afraid of dogs (or any animal with four legs that can just walk freely).

At any rate, I wanted what I wanted and he had the best quality at the best price. So, I was going to meet him.

I told a friend about my upcoming purchase. Instantly, he looked me directly in the eye and said, "That man is going to rape you."

He'd known the man for years. I'd just met him. He insisted I take him with me. I'd been raped before and it was not something I ever wanted to experience again.

As we pulled up to the house, he told me, "You go in first, I will come in later. Don't tell him I am with you."

I did as instructed. When I entered the home, he had a friend there that was equally large in stature, sitting on the couch. The man smiled at me as if he knew me. My stomach began to churn and I felt extremely nervous. The dealer smiled at me and chuckled, making small talk. He asked me why I wasn't in a relationship (this was prior to my husband coming to live with me in Atlanta)… I looked at the coffee table and noticed a black condom package and my stomach churned more.

Suddenly, a shadow passed by the window. The two men instantly moved. "Who is out there?" the dealer asked no one in particular. I just stared at them and didn't say anything. I handed him my money.

Just as quickly my friend came to the door. "What up folk?" he asked in a friendly manner, looking pensively at me.

"Oh it's you, what's up man? I didn't know you were here," the dealer said nervously. He was clearly afraid of my friend, even though my friend was much shorter and smaller in size.

"Yeah, I thought it would be best if I came over here with her, you know," he replied.

The dealer handed me the bag of drugs and we left. In the car, my friend told me to never come over to this dealer's house alone… ever again.

I thanked God for his protection. Even though I was not walking in his will or his way, he still showed me mercy and granted me safety. I didn't deserve it. While I was trying to get to walk a place of letting go of my sinful nature, God didn't desert me. Instead, he honored my efforts and protected me so that I might reach my destination to a place of complete surrender. I was clearly on a path of self-destruction but God preserved me.

*"You have been a shelter for me, a strong tower from the enemy."*
*Psalm 61:3*

## In Context
Let God arise and his enemies be scattered. David wrote the 61st Psalm during a time of great trouble. He was overwhelmed with life and knew his only place of solace, protection and peace was in God's unchanging hand. He finalizes the chapter with 'O prepare mercy and truth which may preserve him – so I will sing praise unto thy name forever and I may perform my vows.'

## Final Notes

No matter where we are in life, as long as we trust God and honor him within our hearts, he will protect us. Just as Asa eventually felt stronger in his own strength and thoughts, we have to be careful about our own progression, profession and confession. It could cost us our lives, especially if we aren't careful to seek the will and help of God in all things.

---

### Prayer

Most Gracious and Heavenly Father, we thank you. We thank you for protecting us from dangers seen and unseen. We thank you for the ability to come before your throne with our greatest concerns for you are a mighty help in the time of trouble. Lord, we will be sure to seek you, quick to listen and steadfast in our obedience to your direction. Please help us to be all that you created us to be and forgive us of our sins.

*In Jesus name we pray, Amen.*

---

**DAY**
# 13

## *The Revelation of Relationship*

*"For the mountains shall depart and the hills be removed, but my kindness shall not depart from you, nor shall my covenant of peace be removed,' says the Lord who has mercy on you."*
*Isaiah 54:10*

### In Context

Spread out and think big! I love this chapter in Isaiah!!! God is saying, don't allow your present condition to convince you that things aren't going to get better. They will and are. You are going to feed nations. You aren't barren, in fact, you will have more children than they who bear children. Yes!!! He further states, that His anger, is but for a moment. He is going to heal, fix and make right every crooked area. He even goes on to say that he is going to build your foundation with sapphire (the strongest gem) and your gates with rubies (the most precious)! He says, 'No weapon that can hurt YOU has EVER been forged... And anyone who openly tries to call you out in court will be dismissed as liars!

### BOOM! SUDDENLY IT HAPPENED.

I was at the Oklahoma State Fair when the rumor hit my ears. We'd just completed a cooking segment with a local gas company and were in the process of finding adorable kids that would be willing to get their faces painted. A coworker came over. Immediately I could see her pleasant, happy-go-lucky disposition was absent. She looked at me with "real" eyes and expressed her concerns. We were being laid off that day. Just as quickly as she whispered it to me, an email about a mandatory meeting held by HR confirmed it. They asked that I come back to the station early.

55

My job was wonderful. I was responsible for our branding, messaging... everything you could see about us externally. The fact that we were being laid off only confirmed I was doing a good job (because from the moment I had my job our number one goal was to improve our value to position ourselves for a good sell)... but at the same time, it was a scary feeling.

I was very comfortable... I had a decent salary, sales commission and the obvious perks a person has when directly related to a television station. It was a comfortable life. Not to mention my personal business was doing well, serving a clientele all over the nation. I couldn't complain.

I have to admit... during that last year I strongly considered taking my business full time. I knew it was becoming an almost uncontrollable desire as it pulled and pulled at me more each day. But... I probably wouldn't have the nerve to 'take the plunge' because I was afraid. I've seen an empty bank account before... that wasn't my greatest fear. Serving with excellence and maintaining brand integrity were. Could I manage the emotional days well while serving clients all day? On a bad day at the office I could always retreat to my secret closet and pray it out... or run out to my car and simply cry it out... but what would I do when I couldn't run away?

The folks at the unemployment office didn't help. They made me face the decision and either embrace or deny the opportunity. It was do or die. They curtly informed me that if I was self-employed (earning any income), I wasn't unemployed. So, either I had to stop operating my business or go find a job. In that moment, I heard God ask me... "Do you trust me?"

"OK GOD! Yes, I trust you but come on now!" I screamed. "This isn't fair!" I cried. No number of tears or incestuous pleading was going to change the situation. I had to make a decision. Did I trust God?

Yes. I did. AND I wanted this. Now I had to take action and believe! But...

I can't sugarcoat it. It was hard. It is hard. Even my mother questioned whether or not I should find a job. "Are you sure?" she asked. I was quick to defend God. "No, I trust Him" I assured her, "God is going to come through!" He did. He has been and just like in the scripture above, he will continue to. But the waiting and the crying and the praying and the hustling and hustling and hustling for work all take place in the middle. It's called the journey.

Now, I may shed a couple tears along the way, but I will smile, laugh and thank God much more… and I plan to leave a legacy and be living proof that GOD is GOD all by himself!

*"Let your conversation be without covetousness; and be content with such things as ye have; for he hath said, I will never leave thee, nor forsake thee. So that we my boldly say, The Lord is my helper, and I will not fear what man shall do unto me."*
*Hebrews 13:5-6*

## In Context

Hebrews 13 shares how we are to interact with others and behave. Knowing that God is our source we must love our neighbor as we love ourselves. Not only must we love our neighbor as we love ourselves but we must honor God. We must honor God with our minds, our mouths and our actions. He strongly encourages us to look to our spiritual leaders and see how they live. To mirror their actions as they should be consistent, honest and open. We should be doers of God's work, not just wearing the label. We should be partnering with him to make positive change in a world that can't or refuses to see him. We have to be in the trenches helping people to meet Jesus and by our actions introduce them to the strength of His love and unending mercy.

## Final Notes

The true revelation of relationship is to honor God with our whole being. We can't offer the fruit of our lips or the works of our hands if our hearts are held or led elsewhere. We have to be wholly committed to Him as he is wholly committed to us. I find that this is a struggle we will face our entire lives. We can commit our lives and still fall astray. We must constantly perform temperature self-checks to see where we are and where we stand. We must worship God in wholeness and in truth as we trust his lead.

---

### Prayer

Dear Lord, forgive us of our sins. Help us to clear our minds and open our hearts to be led by you. We invite your Holy Spirit within to teach and lead us. Lord, strengthen us for this leg of the journey. Your revealed relationship has promised abundance, assurance and accountability. We acknowledge your presence in our lives and bow in complete reverence. Help us to be doers of the word. We thank you for your love, mercy and grace. We thank you for your provision and protection. We thank you for the matchless gift of unblemished life sacrificed for our dirty and unmentionable lives. You are our rock, our shield and our greatest reward.

*In Jesus Name We Pray, Amen.*

# Two Fish and Five Loaves of Bread: God is Able and He Won't Fail

*"And Jesus took the loaves; and when he had given thanks, he distributed to the disciples, and the disciples to them that were set down; and likewise of the fishes as much as they would. When they were filled, he said unto his disciples, Gather up the fragments that remain, that nothing be lost."*
*John 6:11-12*

## In Context

Jesus was in Jerusalem during a feast. On the Sabbath day, he healed a man by the pool of Bethesda. He then spoke about receiving the everlasting gift of eternal life by honoring Him. That those who hear his voice will also hear his voice in the grave. That no amount of knowledge of scripture will save a man. Only honoring Jesus as the savior will save. He goes on to say that while John the Baptist did bear witness of Him, His works were also a witness.

After this, he traveled over the Sea of Galilee and the multitude followed Him across the sea. Then he went to the top of a mountain. (OK, I have to interject here, anyone that heard the Lord speak in Jerusalem and followed him across a sea that spans more than 21 km in length and 13 km in width, then up a mountain is a die-hard fan. They HAD to hear what he had to say.) It was almost time for the feast of Passover. Jesus asked Peter, "How can we feed them?" Peter responded with disbelief, but Andrew noticed a small boy with 2 fish and five loaves of bread. Jesus instructed the men to sit the people down and he prayed over the food while lifting the bread over his head, breaking it and giving thanks. The people had as much as they desired to eat. Then Jesus ordered they gather what was left. After experiencing the miracle, the people were ready to crown him king. But Jesus removed himself and went back inside the mountain alone.

Soon after, the disciples went back down to the sea and began to cross over to Capernaum. In route, the sea rose with a powerful wave in the midst of a storm and the disciples see a figure walking on the water towards them. They were afraid, but it was Jesus. Once in Capernaum, the people that listened to Him speak prior soon arrived. They were surprised to see Him because they knew He didn't get into the boat with the disciples. While in Capernaum, Jesus preached in the synagogues. He explained the value of the bread of life. He knew the people followed because of the miracle they witnessed. But Jesus clarified the value of chasing the real bread of life, Jesus. He explained that soon he would go away and that only by eating his flesh and drinking His blood, often would a person receive eternal life. This was hard for many people to accept… including his disciples. Jesus gave them each an opportunity to leave while openly recognizing one of them would soon betray Him.

### DIVINE PROVISION
When I lived in DC I was broke, broken and always on the verge of my big break. I swallowed 3 years of 401K savings in less than 3 months paying car payments, cell phone bills, buying food and paying 1K a month in rent at the Extended Stay Hotel my children and I lived in. I was desperate and seemingly alone, yet determined.

Before I left Atlanta, I'd started a prayer ministry. I designed and purchased business cards for the ministry. One of them simply read, LOVE. Another read, He Lives, He Knows, He Cares. Another read, HELP! Finally the fourth read, JESUS. Each had a scripture reference and a number for the prayer line. I'd purchased a special line with my cell phone company just for the prayer line.

No one called. No one.

One day, after applying and interviewing with a company, I was called back for a second interview process. I was down to nothing. In order to get to the company, I had to cash in bottles of change at the CompStar change machine at Kroger. After cashing in and putting the meager $2 and change in my gas tank, I nervously headed to the interview. I managed to successfully interview with 7 different team members. It was time for me to head home.

I was in an area I hadn't traveled much and this was before you could access a working map on your cell phone. Even if I could do that, my cell phone had been cut off two days before. I began my trip during heavy traffic, took a wrong exit and ran out of gas. I sat in my car not knowing what to do. I was stranded and lost. I could feel the tears welling up in my eyes. I'd placed the "He lives, He knows, He cares" card in the dash of the car next to the gas tank area. My eyes burned a hole in that card as I swallowed hard.

I was dressed in a 3 piece gray dress suit. I grabbed my laptop bag, locked my doors and began walking. I had no idea where I was going and there was so much traffic. I was trying not to panic. I remember just walking straight ahead. I was walking beneath an overpass, traffic whizzing past me… and I just looked down and forward. I analyzed every piece of gravel and small pieces of debris, broken glass etc.

I didn't make it more than 10 steps before an older black man (maybe mid 50s) pulled over and asked if everything was OK. I told him I was having car trouble. I hesitated then said, "Well I ran out of gas." He looked at me and said, "Get in, I'll take you to get some gas."

I looked into his car. There were beer bottles on the floor in the passenger seat. I remember thinking that this was one of those life choices that could end badly. I looked up at him. He instantly stated, "Well, if you don't have enough for gas, you certainly don't have enough if they tow your car. You stay here and I will go get the gas and come back."

I waited for him to return and he did so within 10 minutes. Once he'd placed the gas in the car, he said "Now I want you to follow me to the gas station so we can put some real gas in this car."

I thanked him and he responded, "No need to thank me! I already love you. You look just like my daughter. Plus I admire your determination." He gave me directions back to the hotel and all was well.

*"He who did not spare His own Son, but delivered Him up for us all, how shall He not with Him also freely give us all things?"*
*Romans 8:32*

### In Context

God's overwhelming love for us is reflected in Romans 8. It speaks of the gift God has provided in eternal life. Its premise is that there is no amount of human effort that can ever be made to earn this gift. In fact, the present sufferings we face as God's children will result in good things that are aligned with our purpose. When we are confused and don't know what to pray, the Holy Spirit will pray for us. Even when we fall short, God's perfect plan will catch us and hold us safely in his presence. Nothing can separate us from God. Nothing!

### Final Notes

God is able. Yes, we may face hard times, but we are never alone or forsaken… we just have to believe that God has a plan and a purpose. He is able to provide our every need… most especially an eternal life with Christ Jesus. In the beginning, the example of feeding the 5,000 shares so many details. First, we must acknowledge there is a need. Second, we must find a resource to supply our needs. Thirdly, we must pray and give thanks. Finally, we must share what we have while being good stewards. In the same way, God has provided Christ as our living bread. We go through the same four steps to receive, accept, worship and share the power of the Gospel of Jesus Christ. God's perfect plan leaves us in a place of unending appreciation.

## Prayer

Most gracious and heavenly Father, we appreciate you. You sent your Son to save us. You provided your Holy Spirit to help us. You are always present with us and in us. We are so thankful. While we are still sinners living in bodies that are insatiable in nature, you still love us. You promised to supply our every need and you never miss the mark. You are always working behind the scenes on our behalf. Lord, where there is need, please send an abundant rain. Where there is trouble, please be present. Where there is danger, please be a fence. Lord, help us to live according to your will. Help us to do what you have assigned. Help us to obey when everything in us wants to disobey. Lord, please keep praying for us when we don't know what to say. Help our words, thoughts and actions align with your purpose for our lives. You are our rock, our shield and our great reward and we thank you.

*In Jesus Name, we pray. Amen*

**DAY 15**

# The Storms of Life

*"And the same day, when the even was come, he saith unto them, Let us pass over unto the other side. And when they had sent away the multitude, they took him even as he was in the ship. And there were also with him other little ships. And there arose a great storm of wind, and the waves beat into the ship, so that it was now full. And he was in the hinder part of the ship, asleep on a pillow: and they awake him, and say unto him, Master, carest thou not that we perish?*

*And he arose, and rebuked the wind, and said unto the sea, Peace, be still. And the wind ceased, and there was a great calm. And he said unto them, "Why are ye so fearful? How is it that ye have no faith?" And they feared exceedingly, and said one to another, "What manner of man is this, that even the wind and the sea obey him?"*
*Mark 4:35-41*

## In Context

Mark chapter 4 begins with Jesus preaching to a group on land as he stood on a boat in the water, away from the crowd. He taught them the parable of Good Seed. Later with the disciples, he better explained the parable and its relationship to the Word of God. He then told his disciples, "Let us go to the other side". I believe this signifies moving forward from one season to the next. In one season, seeds of learning (God's lessons) are imparted and in the next is our testing. On their journey, it reads little ships accompanied them. The waves and water were so high and tumultuous that the disciples began to panic. All the while, Jesus was asleep. (I imagine if the waves were flowing into their boat, they probably witnessed or were witnessing worse with the smaller boats). So, they begged

Jesus to wake up and save them. When he did so, by simply uttering a command, they stood in awe. It was a complete reflection of the lesson he taught just prior to their departure about believing the Word of God (and applying it by activating faith) versus allowing a situation, or fearful/negative surroundings to breed fear.

## A DARK AND STORMY NIGHT… LITERALLY

In April of 2010, I moved into a house with my daughters after a brief period of living with my sister. I was so relieved to finally move in. It was a bad neighborhood, but at least it was home.

The following year, we suffered a couple setbacks. It started when I totaled my beautiful silver Lexus with tinted windows and 20 inch chrome wheels. Shortly after, I booked an extra class during my spring semester and financial aid couldn't cover it. I couldn't afford to pay for the extra class out of pocket and was forced to quit pursuing my Bachelor's degree 9 hours before I could finish… I felt like I was having a Job experience. Every day, something new happened that told me the storm was only going to get worse.

At work, they hired a new manager for the sales department and I was told I was no longer allowed to be a full time employee and make sales commission (but of course I could still sell). I had to watch my co-workers make commission on business relationships I'd worked and developed. It was horrible.

Then my husband and I finalized our divorce… he was engaged within the week.

I started to question God. My younger brother was living with me and I'd just told him the story of Job when all of the problems began. I hated going through all of this and knew somewhere in my mind it was a test. But, I still wondered if God cared about me.

On the evening of May 29, 2012, a storm came. I'd just left a meeting at church. I remember looking out the windows as our meeting came to a close and remarking how ugly it was outside. The vision of cloud cover scared me so much that as I ran out the door, it slammed on the back of my foot and blood rushed to the surface of my heel instantly. I didn't care, I just hurried to my car to get home to my kids.

The storm spanned from 36th and Kelley Avenue to my home on 89th and Broadway Extension. I took photos as I drove (try not to judge me) the entire way home. By the time I arrived on my street, I realized it was going to be one of the most horrific storms I would ever see.

As soon as I got home, I ran in to see where my girls were and what they were doing. Within moments of stepping into the house, I could hear the hail beginning drop. First small tip taps, then stronger and louder thuds, then horrendous cracks. I could hear windows being broken as we huddled inside the small hallway of our home.

The storm was horrific but passed over us leaving only damage to my car. At first, when I looked at the car I was like "Wow, I don't see anything." It did have dents all over it but not much else. Then the next morning as I began to pull out of my driveway, I realized my back window was shattered. It took 7 months before I could replace it. I went everywhere with that shattered window and eventually no window.

The cool thing about the storm… because my car was totaled, I received a large enough check to move my daughters and I out of the neighborhood. I had to choose… either I could move or get my car window fixed and I knew moving was a better choice. My oldest daughter was instantly transferred to a better high school that was within walking distance. My new house was right off the highway and closer to work. It was in a nice, quiet neighborhood with friendly neighbors I could trust.

I was promoted at work to Marketing Coordinator and eventually a new sales manager was hired and I was allowed to work on commission again. I also received two different awards, one for work on our website and another for PR work on one of our shows.

I realized that storms come and go, but in the end, everything

is always OK. There is no need to panic in the storm because
eventually, the sun shines.

*"For his anger endureth but a moment; in his favour is life: weeping may endure
for a night, but joy cometh in the morning."*
Psalm 30:5

## In Context

David's gratitude to God is evident. While he understands that
dark times may arise he starts Psalm 30 with a voice that rings with
appreciation and praise. In the Message Bible, it states, "I give you
ALL the credit…" Then David goes on to describe just how deep of
a mess he was in. He says I yelled for help. Yelled for help. It reminds
me of the man by the gate, screaming "Jesus, Son of David, have
mercy on me!" We have all been there. Even in that moment, when
the Disciples of Christ ignored the man, Jesus responded. I love that
the man by the gate referenced David. God says that David is a "man
after God's own heart". Even when David failed, as this chapter in a
way indicates, he still managed to trust God enough to call on him in
his greatest distress. He begged God to forgive him and God did. In
his favor is life.

## Final Notes

Pain, hardship and struggles are around every corner. Some of them
seem too heavy to bear. Some are self-inflicted and require us to
fall on our faces before God begging for forgiveness. Whether you
have made a mistake, or troubles seem to surround you without
reason, you can depend on God to calm the storms of life. In the
beginning of Mark 4, Jesus breaks down four ways a person can
receive the Word and respond. 1) It's planted on hard ground and
as soon as it is heard it is washed away by evil desires. 2) It's planted
but unfortunately, it has no root… so the minute it gets too difficult,
a person gives up. 3) Surrounded by poor influence. The Word gets
choked by poor surroundings. The final example is the one we all
hope and aspire to achieve. A person has good roots in the Word
of God and believes. Because they believe and don't allow fear to
control them, they obtain their greatest desires!

## Prayer

Lord, we thank you for favor that never leaves us. We thank you
for hearing us when we cry out to you. We know and understand
that are ways are not your ways. So when we have to face a tough
situation, help us to say when we are weak, that we are strong.
Lord, help us to trust you when it appears as though you are asleep
in the middle of our storm. Help us to become the plant that
is watered with your Word and believes it, even when times get
tough. Strengthen us to be your hands and feet even on days when
we need your comfort. Lord, we give you all the glory, all the honor
and all the praise.
*In Jesus name, Amen.*

## *Blessed Assurance*

*"Call to Me, and I will answer you, and show you great and mighty things,*
*which you do not know."*
*Jeremiah 33:3*

### In Context

I am restoring what was destroyed… I will have mercy on them.
This is a reflective statement of God's promise to Jeremiah
concerning Israel and Judah. In anger, God destroyed the city of
Babylonia. So many people were killed that their carcasses littered
the streets and the rubble of destroyed shops and buildings were all
that could be seen. Those that remained were taken into captivity.
Previously, Jeremiah was sent to warn the people, but the king of
Judah, Zedekiah, refused to listen. Rather than change their ways
in obedience to God, they decided to continue in sin. Yet, even
after God completely destroyed the city, he promised Jeremiah, he
was going to rebuild it and make it more beautiful and prosperous
than ever. He promises that His Word to Jeremiah is so certain, that
only if day and night somehow should fall out of their respective
seasons (coming at a time unrecognizable and unpredictable) would
be the only sign that His Word would fail (strongly indicating it was
infallible).

### <u>Doing it MY Way</u>

I have always been very passionate and very head strong. Those are
two aspects of my character I can't seem to shake or get rid of. In
fact, I believe they are wonderful traits to have as God has purposed
me to do great and wonderful things…

But, it hasn't always been a good thing…

When I was 18, driving for about two years, my husband and I traveled the streets of Oklahoma City as though tourists with our last moments ahead of us. We ripped and ran the streets visiting friend to friend, spending the last of our dollars on having a great time.

I, being the one with a better car, drove most often. During our misadventures, I received many a ticket for speeding. My husband, then boyfriend, told me "Don't worry about it. It's not a big deal."

As our adventures continued, the tickets piled up. I think I'd actually gotten up to 4 speeding tickets. During this time, something told me, 'I should care about those tickets. I mean, they give them to you for a reason right?'

At any rate, I was naive and definitely didn't understand the ramifications of punishment ignoring speeding tickets could manifest. Then it happened, I received a warrant for my arrest in the mail.
I initially hid it from my mother. As I recall, the amount listed on the warrant was more than I could afford. I told my brother about it. He warned me, insisting I had to pay it and fast.

Again, I returned to living life as usual. My husband and I loved to party. I moved out of my mother's house and into an apartment with him. We drank and smoked marijuana as if it were going out of style soon. We were living life in YOLO (you only live once) fashion. As if we had nothing to lose.

At the time, he and I worked at the same restaurant. He worked in the back of the house as a cook and I was a waitress. One night, my shift ended early and I didn't want to wait for him. My mother's house wasn't far, I told him to just call me when he was ready to go home. That night, he drove us to work in his stick-shift Datsun. I was still learning to drive the car, but decided I would go for it any way, I was tired.

I was up the street from the apartment complex my mother lived in when I changed lanes at the last minute (moving into the turning lane) without a signal in front of a police car. As I turned the corner, the cop moved behind me and hit the lights, signaling for me to pull over.

After I pulled into the apartments and provided the officer with my license and insurance, I see my brother leaving the apartments in his car. As he passes by my car, he looks at me and mouths, "You are going to jail." My stomach sank.

The woman officer returns to the car and politely informs me that I have a warrant for my arrest and that she was required to take me to jail. I cried and cried but it did not change my situation. Embarrassed, I was placed into hand cuffs and taken to jail.

It was one of the most horrific and wildly interesting nights of my life as so many different women were booked for various offenses throughout the night. There was a woman arrested for selling drugs in a school district – she was actually naked when the cops came and was given some other woman's clothes to wear at her arrival she explained… (she let me sleep on her bunk as the cell was full when I arrived). Another was a 6-months pregnant mother who was arrested for drunk driving (she'd wrapped her car around a pole) and another a thief for stealing from Wal-mart. Later that night women were brought in from a strip club for prostitution (they were the first ones to get out).

I prayed and prayed all night and the next day that I could and would get out of that jail cell soon. When I went to see the judge (via monitor in a hallway) the next day, he curtly informed me that to "work" off my debt I would be in jail for the next 7 days easily. I was devastated.

I continued to pray and ask for forgiveness. I didn't want to spend the next 7 days in jail. I called my mom and asked her to sell my TV (which of course was of little to no value) or to please do whatever she had to do to get the money. I can't remember how she got the funds, but later that afternoon I was released.

I learned my lesson (concerning tickets and speeding). I can't pretend I had this amazing 'Come to Jesus and changed all my ways' moment (that would be a lie), but I can say that I thank God for his mercy and grace not to allow me to spend more time in jail. I slowed down on my bad habits and tried to do better, but 'a hard head always makes for a soft behind' my mother always said.

In this way, I resembled the Babylonians. I was still so head strong and passionate about doing things my way that I stumbled into more and more trouble as life progressed.

The blessed assurance in it all is that God never took his eyes or his hands off of my life. He protected and blessed me along the way, ensuring I learned the necessary lessons needed to bring me into the fulfillment of his purpose for my life. I am still learning every day that I breathe that God is above and beyond merciful. He is loving, consistent and a man of his word.

*"He shall call upon Me, and I will answer him; I will be with him in trouble; I will deliver him and honor him."*
*Psalm 91:15*

## In Context
Psalm 91 reveals the remarkable difference from a believer and a non-believer. God says, "Get to know me and trust me and I will protect you". I love it because he says, when trouble comes, call on me. Not only will I be there with you, I will honor you. I will give you a long life and a long drink of salvation! Those that rest beneath his shadow receive the benefits of protection (from dangers seen and unseen) and a life of peace, absent of fear.

## Final Notes
What a mighty and amazing God we serve! His ways and his thoughts are perfect toward us. While in our ignorance we stumble and fall, He is right there to lift us back up and protect us. He has provided a Savior in Jesus Christ and a Comforter in the Holy Spirit. He has given us a life of peace and knowing that our relationship with him is all that we need in order to survive! Our obedience is birthed in

his blessed assurance and faithfulness. When he protects us, forgives us, dusts of us off and blesses us our only response is gratitude, obedience and faith in Him. When we see a fellow man going through it is our opportunity to testify at the greatness of Jesus, knowing that we too have fallen many times and have been forgiven without fail! His mercy and grace endures forever! He never fails.

---

### Prayer

Oh wonderful Lord and Savior, Jesus, joy fills our hearts as we sing praises to your name. For you are truth in existence, revelation in deed, our shield and our greatest reward. While our love for you may fall short occasion after occasion, your love for us never fails. We are in awe of your grace, amazed by your love and grateful for your presence. You are the lifter of our heads and you remove the cloak of shame. Thank you for the blessed assurance we have in you. Help us to be more like you each day. Help us to make choices that are pleasing in your sight. Grant us wisdom and discernment to do your will in obedience for we know that you prefer obedience to sacrifice. Forgive us and help us to forgive others.

*In Jesus name, Amen.*

DAY
**17**

## *Ordered Steps*

*"The steps of a good man are ordered by the Lord: and he delighteth in his way."*
*Psalm 37:23*

### In Context

Psalm 37 shares an undeniable truth we can embrace wholeheartedly when we have a strong relationship with the Lord… we can trust God. Even when we see people who are evil and seemingly successful surrounding us, we can trust him. Even when things look as though they may go awry, we can trust him.

To ensure we win the race, David presents not only phrases of comfort, but he also shares instruction. Fret not evildoers is married to don't be envious. Trust in the Lord is coupled with do good. Commit thy way is partnered with trust Him. Rest in the Lord is shackled to patience. Cease from anger is twin to forsake wrath.

In all of this, a universal message is being shared… "for yet a little while, and the wicked shall not be: yea, thou shalt diligently consider his place, and it shall NOT be." The battle that we face, isn't ours, but we are to play our position in God's army, trust him and allow him to lead us in the way we should go.

### Desire and Defeat

At the television station, there were 3 designers. Of the three, two were in management. My role was in charge of marketing and public relations: managing our external image via advertising, public relations and social media. The other manager's area was in production, creating set design, program looks and on-air animations.

It was time to redesign our website. I understood the ramifications of creating, editing, functionality and purpose of the site. This was a core responsibility of my role. I also negotiated contracts with the web company and more.

So, when they announced the site was to be redesigned, naturally it became my responsibility. However, the other manager took it upon herself to insist, she redesign the site. Management considered her idea and allowed her to submit her designs and thoughts. I too was to work up a design.

Leading up to the presentation of our ideas, you would think she already won based on her actions and words. I didn't say anything, I just prayed, designed and redesigned until I was happy with the result. I called our partners to find out what was possible and if my ideas could really be implemented with the design. I just worked hard.

The day of our revealing to management, she was so excited to submit her plans. I was nervous and prayed my overall look and feel, analysis and basis for structure, functionality and background design would go over well. She brought in the other designer as her backup. He agreed with her suggestions without ever asking to see my design or hear my suggestions. He even submitted reasoning as to why her look was amazing.

We all listened patiently as she presented. The site was beautiful but did not speak to the core of our brand, our audience and was not designed for scalability. They liked her design and allowed me to present.

I created a series of handouts to explain the design and functionality. I also knew our goals for the future and explained how they could seamlessly integrate into the sites design. I also presented options we hadn't discussed but should consider, explaining their value to the overall site.

The result was obvious. They overwhelmingly decided my design was the one to go with. After implementation of our site, at the National Association of Broadcasters convention, our site was used by the company that created it as an example of what they could do for broadcast stations all over the nation. I also won an award for site design from the Society of Professional Journalists.

*"For the vision is yet for an appointed time; But at the end it will speak, and it will not lie. Though it tarries, wait for it; Because it will surely come, It will not tarry."*
*Habakkuk 2:3*

## In Context
Habakkuk breaks it down. He shares that the writing is on the wall for evil doers. That while they are drunk with their own self-righteousness they are also oblivious to the truth that surrounds them. God also instructs the believer to place the writing on the wall and make it plain. So plain, that a person running past it would be able to see it and absorb it.

## Final Notes
In our lives we will always suffer from the vision of those that are not walking with God but seem to be so successful. In all of this God says to be patient, to wait for HIS move. It's coming and it will not be late. He is faithful. He has ordered our steps so that our destiny will be fulfilled according to His will and way. He is working His strategic plan for your life. You can rest in God, knowing that your day and time are coming. In the meantime, don't be angered to wrath, don't be envious, commit yourself to God and do good. Write the vision and make it plain, knowing that in due season you will reap what you sow.

### Prayer

Thank you Lord for reminding us of your sovereignty in all things. Thank you for blessing us with ears to hear your Word as it comes forth. Protect us oh God from our enemies and help us to trust you in the full silence that beckons our response. Your ways are not ours. Help us to trust your character when we can't see you moving. Teach us to pray for our enemies. Teach us to forgive. Teach us to lean not to our own understanding but in all of our ways, to truly acknowledge you.

*Lord, please continue to order our steps. In Jesus name, Amen.*

# Abundant Life, Love and Laughter

*"When the ruler of the feast had tasted the water that was made wine, and knew
not whence it was: (but the servants which drew the water knew;) the governor of
the feast called the bridegroom, And saith unto him, Every man at the beginning
doth set forth good wine; and when men have well drunk, then that which is
worse: but thou hast kept the good wine until now. This beginning of miracles did
Jesus in Cana of Galilee, and manifested forth his glory;
and his disciples believed on him."*
*John 2:9-11*

## In Context

Turning water into wine. Jesus was still a young adult when his
mother Mary approached him in distress. She knew her son was
anointed to do great work in the kingdom and Jesus knew it was
for an appointed time. While the situation itself, a celebration of
commitment to a life of serving one another, was symbolic for the
life Jesus so quickly and seamlessly dedicated himself to by becoming
the bridegroom, there is an overt sensitivity to the fact that Jesus was
unaware his season was no longer a future thing but a present thing.
(Think on that.) While Jesus questioned his mother's request, she
insisted the servants do whatever he said to do.

Immediately after the wedding and the miracle of turning water into
wine, Jesus takes his position as bridegroom and enters a sanctuary
that is no longer serving its purpose. He begins to overturn the tables
and kick out those that were using the church as a marketplace. He
immediately began to operate in his season.

## IT WAS GOOD… AND THEN IT WAS EXCELLENT

As a designer, I will never starve. It's true. You can't look around your house without seeing a designers work. Try it. Look around. Your mail, your clothing, your television, your books… design is everywhere.

One of the ways God blessed me was to take me on a specific journey concerning my career. Initially, I spent over 10 years in customer service (the core to any person's professional success no matter the field or position). Then, he placed me into a mesh pot of creative learning in a technology center that was more like a candy store for me… if I wanted to learn it, I could. After, he placed me in the marketplace to truly "learn" what I'd been taught beyond foundation, he thrust me into application. Once I mastered design, he infused my passion, by pushing me into creative writing and event focused messaging for business. Finally, after "preparing me (which he is still doing more and more each day)" he placed me into servant leadership.

This specific journey in my career coupled with my personal life experiences have pushed me into passionate, purpose-driven living and require a commitment to serve God with all of me. Not just my mind and heart, but with my hands and feet too!

The path God has placed me on started as a good path: consistent work, good income and a good life. But, what his preparation and heart work have allowed for is an excellent life, which I have learned, only comes with a disciplined and relational obedience to God.

*"And it shall come to pass, if thou shalt hearken diligently unto the voice of the Lord thy God, to observe and to do all his commandments which I command thee this day, that the Lord thy God will set thee on high above all nations of the earth: And all these blessings shall come on thee, and overtake thee, if thou shalt hearken unto the voice of the Lord thy God."*
*Deuteronomy 28:1-2*

## In Context

A land that flows with milk and honey. This is the premise Moses began in Deuteronomy 27 to teach the Israelites. He explained the importance of honoring the law and distinguished the difference between the blessing and the curse. This teaching is expanded in Deuteronomy 28. Both books truly provide valuable wisdom and insight into the keys of abundant life. They describe in great detail, what will and what won't bless, protect and keep you. The laws in the Old Testament still hold true today and are God's promise.

## Final Notes

Your "Excellent" season is always now. We just miss recognizing it sometimes. In John 2, the chapter shares so many key messages, I would be remiss not to share them.

### 1) SAVING THE BEST FOR LAST

Your today is always your best season, even if it doesn't feel that way, you are being prepared for your highest and best use.

### 2) A LIFE OF COMMITMENT

You must commit to something, it will either be self or God but you can't choose both.

### 3) SERVING IS A TWO-WAY STREET

Jesus is a committed mate always serving his people. In a committed relationship, it must be mutually beneficial. God does not require much but he does require commitment and service.

### 4) OBEDIENCE RENDERS UNBELIEVABLE RESULTS

When we obey God (regardless of what it looks like to others – consider Noah), we are blessed beyond reasoning or imagination… simply because we chose to trust and obey.

### 5) GOD'S TIMING IS PERFECT AND REVEALED IN AN INSTANT

Our recognition will only come if we are in a real relationship with God allowing us to not only recognize but also embrace our season with obedient action.

### Prayer

Lord, we give you all the glory! You are a perfect God, knitting us together for the perfect work you have created us to do. We choose to fully embrace our season with laughter and joy. Regardless of where we are in the journey, we are committed to obey, trust and love your perfect direction and plan. Pour your wisdom, patience and efficiency into the foundation of our beings to excellently serve in the great works which you have predestined us to do. As we walk, hold our hands and whisper the words we need to keep moving forward in strength. Thank you for your love. Thank you for your mercy. Thank you for your grace. Above all, we thank you for committing to see us through to the end working a perfect patience and love that will last forever.

*In Jesus Name we pray, Amen.*

# Mistaken Identity

*"He saith unto them, But whom say ye that I am? And Simon Peter answered
and said, Thou art the Christ, the Son of the living God. And Jesus answered
and said unto him, Blessed art thou, Simon Barjona: for flesh and blood hath not
revealed it unto thee, but my Father which is in heaven. And I say also unto thee,
That thou art Peter, and upon this rock I will build my church; and the gates of
hell shall not prevail against it. And I will give unto thee the keys of the kingdom
of heaven: and whatsoever thou shalt bind on earth shall be bound in heaven: and
whatsoever thou shalt loose on earth shall be loosed in heaven."*
*Matthew 16:15-19*

## In Context

Matthew 16 begins with the Pharisees & Saducees demanding a sign
from Jesus to prove that he was indeed from heaven. Jesus' response
was that a wicked adulterous nation requires signs. Then he warned
his disciples to watch out for the false teachings of Pharisees and
Saducees. This led him to ask them, "Whom do men say I the Son
of Man am?" He received many responses but only Peter referred to
him as the Christ and Son of the Living God.

Jesus immediate response to Peter was a description I believe for any
man that truly believes Jesus is the Son of God and our savior. He
told him he was blessed and that his revelation came from the Spirit
of God. He told him that he was the ROCK upon which he would
build his church (that the gates of hell would not prevail against
it). He also promised him the keys to the kingdom of heaven and
pronounced that whatever he decreed (bound or loose) in heaven

and earth would be happen in heaven and earth. We are the church: the foundation for believers. We are blessed. We are the hands and feet of Christ. We are doing great works by fighting a battle based on the decree of our lips; having the ability and power to bind and loose situations in heaven and earth.

Jesus then explained that he would be leaving them soon. Peter said "no" and opposed what he said. Jesus responded with "Get thee behind me Satan."

**SHE THOUGHT SHE KNEW ME...**
At the television station, there seemed to always be a revolving door of sales managers. In 4 years, we had 7 sales managers and occasionally went months without a manager. It was a very demanding position that required results. No amount of talking could change the measuring stick used to reflect performance.

During my last couple of months at the station, a new sales manager was hired. She was rude, abrasive and demanding... and she thought she knew me. Immediately, I noticed she had something against me, often making discouraging or disparaging remarks about me.

Many times I tried to have a meeting of the minds with her. I would go out of my way to try and please her but still to no avail.

Then, she began stalking me on social media. She would look at my linked in profile every day. She would comment on my posts in passing and one day, she even went so far as to say, "So you own a marketing company... well if you own a company, you should do this better."

I knew I was just a hot button for her blow off steam. She'd never been a manager before and needed someone to release the sudden amount of pressure she was feeling. She needed to point out that someone was worse than she was.

As time went on, it only got worse. I would often go in the bathroom to pray, which has always been my secret place. One day, the anger had risen so far up within me that as I sat on the bathroom floor, I began to wail. Loudly. People could hear it in the hallway. I couldn't make it stop. It began as a prayer but ended with something even I didn't recognize.

The HR director came in to speak with me. I had never in my career behaved this way and thought it was a clear reflection on me. I hated it.

When I got into her office, I explained my frustration. I told her, I was doing my best to respect her but it was not easy. In fact, it only got more and more difficult each day.

The HR director admitted to me that she too had to go to management about this woman because she belittled her as well. She told me that she'd never been treated that way and had to go to the president about it (the day they hired her).

She told me not to worry and to take the rest of the day off.

Friendship comes over time. Respect grows over time. I would like to say that we eventually developed a friendship and great working relationship, but we just didn't have the time... all I can say is, she thought she knew me.

*"The Pharisees therefore said unto him, Thou bearest record of thyself; thy record is not true. Jesus answered and said unto them, Though I bear record of myself, yet my record is true: for I know whence I came, and whither I go; but ye cannot tell whence I come, and whither I go. Ye judge after the flesh; I judge no man."*
*John 8:13-15*

## In Context
Jesus was approached by the Pharisees with a woman who committed adultery. They gathered around her with stones in hand, ready to administer her prescribed punishment. However, there is clearly no record of the man she committed adultery with. Jesus then charged, them: "He that is without sin cast the first stone." When everyone

left he forgave the woman and charged her to stop sinning.

Later he preached, "I am the light – no one who follows me stumbles in darkness." Then the argument began with Pharisees insisting that because he alone provided the testimony that it was a lie. Jesus then asserted, you judge based on what you see and touch, I don't. But, even if I did, my judgment would be fair and based on what God says. "My father is my witness." Then they asked who his father was and he responded, "You are looking right at me and don't even know me." He then insisted if they can't see God in him, they don't know God. Then they asked, "Who are you anyway?" But his response was, "If you don't believe me, you really don't believe the one who sent me." But the religious leaders didn't understand. So he further iterated, "The one who sent me stays with me. He doesn't abandon me. He sees how much joy I take in pleasing him."

Jesus then turned to the believers and said, "If you stick with this, living out what I tell you, you are my disciples for sure. Then you will experience for yourselves the truth, and the truth will free you." They questioned him, desiring clarity regarding freedom they thought they already had and fatherhood (Abraham vs. God). The Jews thought all his talk was crazy and influenced by the devil. But, Jesus corrected them by saying, "Verily, verily I say unto you, if a man keep my saying, he shall never see death." This sent them into another rant insisting he thought he was better than their father, Abraham.

In this he responded, "If I honor myself, my honor is nothing. It is my father that honors me, of whom you say, that he is your God. Yet you don't know him, I know him. If I said I didn't know him, I would be a liar, but I know him and I do what he says." Then he added, "Before Abraham was, I am."

## Final Notes
Often times we are the victims of mistaken identity. Sometimes we mistake others. Many people questioned who Jesus was and many were confused. As ambassadors of Christ, we can lead by his example. It starts with mercy and grace. If we can be forgiven, surely

we can forgive others. If we are walking with God, we know what he reveals to us is true. We must trust God and be obedient even when it seems like we are in a season of me against the world. We must also understand that everyone won't recognize us as ambassadors of Christ, regardless, we must still walk the walk. God promises if we do so, allowing him to honor us when the time is right, we will never see death. That is a promise worth fighting for.

---

**Prayer**

Lord, help us to honor you when times are tough. Help us to be a light in a dark world. Help us to honor your word and live as you decree. You promised us that if we honor you and serve you, you would give us the keys to the kingdom of heaven helping us to bind and loose what is good in your eyesight. Thank you Lord for forgiving us of every sin, help us to extend the grace we have received. Lord, we love you and trust you. We give you all the glory and the praise.

*In Jesus Name, Amen.*

## DAY
## 20

# Never Give Up!

*"And let us not be weary in well doing, for in due season we shall reap
if we faint not."*
*Galatians 6:9*

### In Context

The Message Bible opens this book with the following three words,
"Live creatively, friends." It is the crux of operating based on faith.
This book screams two things to me... one, be humble and two,
serve God's people. It teaches us to forgive, chase our God given
purpose, to understand that we reap what we sow, be doers of the
word and not a broken mirror (reflecting what is not real or true) and
to never give up on God.

### HE TOLD ME TO DO IT

Holding programs for women and teens can be difficult. But, it is
one of the things I have been called to do. Every program I have
ever launched, whether it is KYSE: Kiss Your Self-Esteem, She's a
BOSSE or Grindaholix has tested my faith in more than one way.
In my first program, KYSE, my financing fell through two weeks
before the launch. I was afraid. I cried. I yelled. I prayed. The only
thing I heard from God was, "Have faith."

During our first She's a BOSSE Etiquette Clinique, finances were so
tight, our water was cut off for 3 days. There were tears shed during

this process as well. It was a horrible experience.

For Grindaholix, I was challenged in every way, from speakers fighting with caterers and having to fill both spots at the last minute to having a serious lack of enrollment.

This year, I am planning the largest etiquette Clinique ever for She's a BOSSE. It is really ambitious and I know so many young ladies are going to be blessed. But it too, is a serious test of my faith. To believe for resources, enrollment, commitment and the fulfillment of every promise I have made is never an easy walk and demands crazy faith in God to bring HIS vision to pass. But, I refuse to give up. I know this is what God has ordained and that it is HIS vision, so whatever is needed will be provided. Whatever is done is according to HIS will.

I move forward in faith, trusting him to provide every need… because He told me to do it. He has never let me down nor given me a reason to give up.

*"So neither he who plants nor he who waters is anything, but only God who gives the growth."*
*I Corinthians 3:7*

## In Context

I Corinthians 3 shares a strong truth. We are all simply playing our part in God's big plan. So many times we consider the work that we do to be the be-all, end-all of what God has assigned. But, he is very clear in this: one plants, one waters but only God brings the growth. If we aren't working with a clear understanding that a person's growth or salvation will never and has never come directly from us (that in fact we were just invited to be a part of the process), then we are only fooling ourselves. The truth, as Paul relates, is that if we build under any other understanding the thing we built will be destroyed. It won't work. We will survive to serve another day, but that "creation" will not.

**Final Notes**

Thank God for his vision. If God has placed something on your heart to do, do so with gladness. You can't look at your resources, support or the rationality of what you believe. You have to keep moving in faith, knowing what God desires, He will bring to pass. We are all assigned specific positions and our only responsibility is to play our part.

---

### Prayer

Jesus, you are the author and finisher of our faith. We thank you for vision, direction, clarity and provision. Lord, please remove anything that is not like you from our hearts and our minds. Help us to prepare for your works according to your will and your way. Please help us to be everything you have created us to be and to serve you in wholeness and truth. Forgive us and help us to forgive others. Direct our paths and make it straight.

*In Jesus Name, Amen.*

---

# Go Tell It on the Mountain!

*"How beautiful upon the mountains are the feet of him that bringeth good tidings, that publisheth peace; that bringeth good tidings of good, that publisheth salvation; that saith unto Zion, Thy God reigneth!"*
*Isaiah 52:7*

## In Context

Isaiah 52 is a message from God boasting about the great salvation of his people. He begins by explaining that all that boast of God's goodness are beautiful. He also shares that those that have no time or desire for God are dismissed. He then tells the story of oppression against those that honor God. Much like the life and story of many greats (David/Joseph), God's people are first born into slavery, then oppressed, then spoken evil of and finally free. Not only are they free, they are eternal heirs to God's victorious life. He says that we are free to go, but we must be clean and free. Pure from evil. That we don't have to run to victory. He is leading us and has our back. He finalizes the book with a boastingly proud testimony of Jesus. Noting that many will see his disfigured face, evidence of a life of accusations and assault, and be appalled at his physical appearance... but his beautiful glory and grace will stand tall and proud as King of Kings and Lord of Lords.

## UGLY BEGINNINGS AND BEAUTIFUL ENDINGS

God has blessed me and I have always had his favor in my life. I haven't always recognized it though.

As a child I was molested by a family friend. As a teenager, I saw a friend die by gunfire. As an adult, I lost a child due to making a poor rushed decision in an emotional state (I had an abortion). I separated from my husband and was subsequently raped. I became a drug addict.

Life seemed to throw me curve ball after curve ball. A lot of it happened because I chose to do life on my terms. I didn't know that God kept my rapist from killing me. That God was protecting me from being in the wrong place at the wrong time on so many nights I sought to purchase drugs. I didn't know I had to see a man die of gang violence to keep me from pursuing stronger ties and alliances to the gang. That he ended a molester's ability to rape me over and over again by allowing my parents to get divorced.

No, I couldn't recognize his favor. I didn't see his protection. I didn't understand what he was trying to teach me. I couldn't see my today yesterday. Yet, all of these experiences... as horrible as the memories are and as painful as the heartbeats of regret may thump... helped to shape me into the person I am today.

I don't look at people like others do. When I see a homeless person, I wonder what order of life altering events brought them to that place and how I can make today better. When I see a person who is seemingly judged based on their dress or attitude, I ponder their personal reflections of self-love or guilt. I think I am beginning to see as Jesus sees.

Each person is valuable. Like a crumpled and torn dollar bill still has value, each of us still holds value and purpose. We were destined to impact someone's life. When God reached down to save me, I couldn't imagine why. I felt like it was all over... hopeless.

God gave me a life that is hope full. I only hope the sharing of my seediest tales can expose someone to the overwhelming power of God's ability to save... of his selfless example of unending grace and his incomparable ability to extend mercy.

*"Don't talk about this all over town. Just quietly present your healed body to the priest, along with the appropriate expressions of thanks to God. Your cleansed and grateful life, not your words, will bear witness to what I have done."*
Matthew 8:4, Message Bible

## In Context

All throughout Matthew 8, we see Jesus healing the sick. He heals leprosy, the deathly ill, saves the lives of those tossed at sea… happy to save and happy to heal. Yet, early in the chapter after he heals the man with leprosy, he clearly instructs him not to tell. Instead, he says to let his LIFE be the testimony. It is so powerful. So profound. Again, in this chapter, Jesus unpacks so much about the believer and a life of healing. He teaches about blind faith in the command of God (the captain of the army & the disciples at sea) and his ability to heal without recognition of demonic activity or the presence of illness (leper and Peter's mother in law).

## Final Notes

We are blessed when we give God the glory he deserves. We are all in the process of being made more like him each day (whether we realize it or not) because he is always doing a perfect work in our lives to help us be the best we can be. The Lord wants us to run and tell the world how wonderful and great the gift of salvation is. He also wants us to take it further by being sure to SHOW the world with our actions and not just give lip service. Both share the same message in compelling ways and reflect an undeniable truth. God is amazing and his love for us will never fail. Not only is he at work in our today, he has already carved a path of greatness for our tomorrows.

### Prayer

Most Gracious and Heavenly Father, we thank you for the gift of life that is so precious in your sight. While we may not recognize the beautiful gifts of protection, mercy and grace that you provide each day, help us to testify and believe in blind faith that you are working it out for our good. Lord, help us to share your wonderful blessings with the world around us. Not only in word, but also in deed. Help us to extend love, to be love and to recognize love. Lord, strengthen us for our journey as your servants and direct us as only you can.

*In Jesus Name, Amen.*

DAY
**22**

# The Debt is Paid

*"And every one that was in distress, and every one that was in debt, and every one that was discontented, gathered themselves unto him; and he became a captain over them: and there were with him about four hundred men."*
1 Samuel 22:2

## In Context

David was anointed to be king. But, before he was able to take his place on the throne, the current king Saul was on a manhunt for his life. David, forced to seek refuge ran to hide in a cave. Many that were in debt or unhappy with current conditions (in the kingdom) followed him, vowing their alliance and support. David, understanding the true threat of danger, to not only himself, but also his family sought separate safety for them with the King of Moab. After, David went to visit a compound of priests for spiritual guidance and protection. The priests advised him, prayed for him and gave him the sword of Goliath. When Saul heard about the priests and what they'd done, he traveled to Nob to confront them. The priests responded with a statement of validity, "There's not an official in your administration as true to you as David, your own son-in-law and captain of your bodyguard. None more honorable either. Do you think that was the first time I prayed with him for God's guidance? Hardly! But don't accuse me of any wrongdoing, me or my family. I have no idea what you're trying to get at with this 'outlaw' talk." After which, Saul had all the priests at Nob killed by his servant, an Edomite.

## Good Intentions, Horrible Outcomes

Nothing hurts more than to see all of your effort, dedication and hard work taken for granted or even worse, resented. But, it happens all of the time, all over the world for reasons we can't seem to understand or explain.

As a parent, we work tirelessly for our children. We want to help our children become whole, successful, healthy, servants to God. We often go out of our way to ensure they have everything they need to succeed. Our advice may fall on deaf ears, be seen as overbearing or even worse, be ignored all together.

As my daughter prepared to attend college, I advised her to take things slow and seriously. I explained the importance of meeting deadlines and following up. I told her to develop relationships with financial aid staff, professors and leaders. To each word of advice, I was met with the same set of comments: 'I know, I am on it', or 'Mama, you don't have to tell me that', or 'I am working on that'. No matter the advice, she 'already' knew what she needed to do.

A day arrived and I could tell my daughter was in great distress. She suffers from anxiety and I could see she was feeling overwhelmed. I asked, "Can I help?"
"No, it's OK. I am just a little stressed."

I began to worry. I knew it had to be big based on her level of anxiety. But I backed off to avoid a big outburst. I began to consider my leadership in her life as led by example. Was I a person that refused help? YES. Was I a person that was filled with pride and rather have utilities shut off than let others know I was drowning? YES.

This concerned me. I wanted my daughter to reach out for help, but how often had I shown her that toughing it out and doing it on your own was the "right" way?

I began to pray and ask God to help me. I soon learned that God's help meant that I would have to re-teach, help her accept help and learn it all at the same time myself. My daughter eventually had to leave college and move back home. We are starting over and it is all going to work out in due season.

I am still learning, but thank God we have second chances.

*"Shouldest thou not also have had compassion on thy fellow servant, even as I had pity on thee?"*
*Matthew 18:33*

## In Context

Matthew 18 is a reflection on forgiveness and humility. Jesus instructs his disciples to be as humble as children and to treat others with fairness. He further issues, if you are prone to sin it is better to prune that thing from you than keep it and be cast into a lake of fire. Then he starts to speak about disagreements among others and forgiveness. His last example is of a man forgiven for much but refuses to forgive others. But, his debt had been paid so why not forgive? Jesus finishes the chapter with the following: "So likewise shall my heavenly Father do also unto you, if ye from your hearts forgive not every one his brother their trespasses."

## Final Notes

We all need help from time to time. Even when we are doing our best we can fall into trouble and need help. We have to first understand that this is normal and the way God designed us. We were never intended to be fully self-sufficient. We all need help from time to time. Not only do we need help, we also need forgiveness. There is not a person walking this earth that hasn't desired forgiveness for a mistake. Jesus paid for our debts with his life, not just his earthly life but his everlasting life as well. From the beginning, he formed the earth and all in it. He created us in his likeness and sacrificed his earthly life. He is praying for each of us now as we walk in his will and in his way. He is the captain of our souls, our shield and our greatest reward.

**Prayer**

Only you Lord, know our inner workings and thoughts. You know every situation before we find ourselves there. You are our beginning and our end, our Alpha and our Omega. Lord, help us to be humble enough to ask for help and strong enough to forgive. Help us to seek your will in every situation and trust in you. We thank you Lord. We give you praise Lord. We honor you Lord. We magnify you Lord!

*In Jesus Name we pray, Amen.*

# When We Stop Doing and Start Listening

*"He that hath an ear, let him hear what the Spirit saith unto the churches."*
*Revelations 3:22*

**In Context**

In Revelations 3, a letter is written to each of the churches in Sardis, Philadelphia and Laodicea. To Sardis, God warns: I see you working but not for me. I know that you are busy but you are focused in the wrong direction. Return to what you heard originally and work in your purpose. To Philadelphia, He assures: I have seen you working hard to keep my word. Even when it was hard for you, you still believed. There are many that call themselves righteous but aren't being real. Hold on to your crown tightly and don't allow distractions to pull you away. When all is said and done, I will exalt you before them and all will know who really worshipped me in wholeness and truth. To Laodicea, God warns: Get it together. You teeter totter between good and evil but it would be much better if you make a choice to be one or the other. I am here because I love you and I want the best for you. Listen, I am standing at the door knocking. If you let me in, I will come in and eat with you. At my table, I sit among conquerors… Because only conquerors sit at the table in a place of honor. Just as I have conquered and sit at the side of my Father.

## LONELY, LOST AND LISTENING

As a single parent working hard, you can feel down and lonely. It's hard bearing all of your burdens, all of your good times and all of your concerns with God alone. Any single woman needs a close circle of friends she can trust to share these concerns with.

Unfortunately, not all women have that. I for one, have serious issues with trust. It is difficult for me to trust others and as a result, I often share my hurts and successes with everyone, anyone or just God. It varies depending on the issue.

At any rate, I find that I am often "misplacing" my crown because I am distracted by great opportunities in business, possible relationships or fear of failure (so I am making poor choices).

I met a young man (21 years of age) who for whatever reason was absolutely smitten with me. For months I ignored him. I was just flattered and moved on. One day, after an argument with a man I'd been dating, I saw this young man at Bible Study. He was just as persistent as always except this time, I gave him my telephone number.

Well, before you know it, we would talk on the phone for hours or text back and forth all day. I was meeting him at his job. He was coming over my house. Soon, a relationship developed. Was I seriously considering having a relationship with this young man? It was ridiculous.

I lost my crown somewhere in the madness of being lonely… of being rejected by someone I loved greatly. As I realized my state, I began to cry and beg God to help me. I was spiraling down a path of destruction and felt hopeless.

That's when I heard him whisper, "Just listen to me and stop moving. You are doing too much too quickly without waiting to hear for my direction or instruction."

*"And the Lord came, and stood, and called as at other times, Samuel, Samuel.
Then Samuel answered, Speak; for thy servant heareth."*
I Samuel 3:10

## In Context

Samuel was a gift from God to his mother Hannah. She dedicated his life to the service of God and as a result, he lived in the church with Eli, the prophet. But, Eli had 3 sons, who were supposed to be groomed to serve in the ministry, but instead were vagrants in the street behaving inappropriately, disrespecting God and the church (and Eli knew about it). One night, God approaches Samuel while he is sleeping. He calls his name. Samuel, assuming it was Eli, runs to his bedside. Eli assures him he did not call his name. Samuel returns to bed, only to be awakened again as he hears his name being called. Again he returns to Eli's bedside to serve. Again, Eli says, "It was not me". Finally, upon a third return, Eli realizes and tells him, "It is the Lord. The next time he calls you, respond with 'Speak Lord, for your servant is listening'." Samuel does as instructed and God begins to share a detailed prophecy concerning Eli's sons and the unfortunate fall of Eli's family. The next morning Eli insists Samuel share the message from God with him. Reluctantly, Samuel shares the message exactly as it is given. Eli has no choice but to respect God's decision.

## Final Notes

We need to be receptive and ready to hear the Lords voice at all times. Whether it is for correction, direction or revelation, we need to be listening. Often times, life can distract us, discourage us and dissuade us from being a listening vessel. Out of God's belly flow rivers of living water. He never gets tired of teaching, leading and protecting us. We just need to develop a new thirst for his instruction, his Word and his Spirit. When times get tough and we find ourselves falling down a path of destruction, we need to take a moment and hear from God BEFORE we make our next move and lose our precious crowns.

## Prayer

Lord Jesus, please God, open our hearts and minds to hear your voice. Help us to seek you in our times of trouble, restlessness and loneliness. Help us to seek you while you may be found and help us to hold on to your unchanging hand as the winds of life toss us to and fro. Lord, help us to recognize your knock, be willing to open the door and enjoy your presence as we bask in your knowledge, grace and love. Lord, please forgive us of our sins and help us to be better to others as you always give your best to us.

*In Jesus Name we pray, Amen.*

# Faith. Action. Trust.

*"Knowing this, that the trying of your faith worketh patience."*
*James 1:3*

## In Context

James Chapter 1 is a beast. James is breaking it down for believers. He is holding us accountable to the words we speak and claim to believe. He lets us know the product of faith is walked out right in front of us. Believers who are walking in faith understand how powerful the combination of faith, action and trust is.

### LISTENING TO GOD AND BEING OBEDIENT

When I was 27 years old, I'd left my husband of 8 years to move into an apartment with my two daughters. During that time, I was drugged and raped by a man I met online.

The man kept calling me after the rape. It drove fear into my heart.

My brother lived in Atlanta for several years by then and my sister recently moved there. I was stuck in Oklahoma with an ex-husband who refused to get right, a close friend I greatly admired living in Chicago and a rapist that thought it was adventurous to keep calling the woman he raped.

One day, I heard God whisper, "Move to Atlanta."

Now, I'd just been promoted to an outstanding job, was making enough money to take care of myself and children and was finally financially comfortable. Moving seemed crazy. BUT, the rapist did scare me. He knew where I lived and could come over at any time… and I certainly didn't want that to happen, especially with children at home.

I gave one month notice at my job. I'd explained what happened and what I'd decided. I didn't even have a job lined up. God gave me a plan and I worked it. I got shot records, dental checks, eyes checked – everything. I called one of the guys I met in Chicago at the conference. He lived in Atlanta and asked him if he knew of any openings. Fortunately, they had one in his office.

I rented a car, drove to Atlanta, interviewed for the job and got it. I then went to find an apartment. I was pleased I found one in the same complex my brother and sister lived in, right next door. It was all in God's will.

Two years to the day of our separation, I moved to Atlanta. It was a seamless transition. All because I listened, trusted God and took action. What if I chose to ignore or disbelieve God?

*"…Nevertheless, when the Son of Man cometh shall he find faith on earth?"*
*Luke 18:8b*

**In Context**
Luke 18 begins with a parable of a woman who refused to let a judge forget her justice. The judge was not man of God but was tired of the woman's insisting. Jesus used the parable as a parallel to the prayers of a believer, ensuring God would not ignore the fervent prayer of the righteous. He then transitioned to another parable about authentic prayer. His story involved to men praying in the open. One of them recited a prideful prayer he'd prayed plenty of times, another prayed from his heart full of humility. The man with honest and humble prayer was respected by God.

Then some of the people wanted to bring their babies to be healed but the disciples turned them away. Jesus then explained that the children should always be welcomed, and that in fact, the only believers that would enter heaven would have to believe as little children.

A man asked, "Good Master, what must I do to enter heaven?" To which Jesus insisted that there is only one that is good and that is God. He then told the man to sell all of his goods and give the pay to the needy, then to take up his cross and follow Jesus. The man was sad and Jesus responded at how difficult it would be for the rich to enter heaven.

When questioned, his response was, "What is impossible with man is possible with God." The disciples had given up everything they had to follow Jesus. He assured them that they would receive far more than what was sacrificed in this life and the next.

Finally, they left for Jerusalem as Jesus shared his fate to come. While traveling, they approached Jericho and there was a blind man begging, "Thou Son of David, have mercy on me!" Jesus asked him what he desired. The man answered that he might see. Jesus responded, "Receive thy sight, thy faith has saved thee."

**Final Notes**
Faith. Action. Trust. Son of David, Have Mercy on Me! This line has impacted me greatly ever since I saw it performed at a play. The man bellowed the words from his heart and it pricked me in mine. How many times are we placed in situations where only prayer, faith and those activating steps can get us out? Plenty. God has never failed us and he never will. If you have heard him give you a directive, it is time you stepped out in faith and moved forward. Don't allow fear to keep you from aligning with his purpose.

Prayer

Most gracious and heavenly Father, strengthen us with peace as we learn the value of patience. Help us to stand in faith, trusting you at your word. Direct our paths and help us to align our footsteps with your will. Teach our hands to work as you see fit. Help us to invest in your directives, trust in your provision, bless with your authority and stand still in grace as we wait for you. Lord we trust, believe and have faith in you and only you.

*In Jesus Name we pray, Amen.*

# On the Brightest Day

*"For unto us a Child is born,*
*Unto us a Son is given;*
*And the government will be upon His shoulder.*
*And His name will be called*
*Wonderful, Counselor, Mighty God,*
*Everlasting Father, Prince of Peace.*
*Of the increase of His government and peace*
*There will be no end,*
*Upon the throne of David and over His kingdom,*
*To order it and establish it with judgment and justice*
*From that time forward, even forever.*
*The zeal of the Lord of hosts will perform this."*
*Isaiah 9:6*

## In Context

Isaiah 9 proclaims a time of eternal bright victory over seasons of darkness. "Unto us a child is born!" This child is going to bring peace and glory that will reign where blood stained banners and tyrant employers once ruled. It is the prophecy of a Savior born to save us all. Then Isaiah warns of impending doom. Israel has gone her own way to do her own thing. Isaiah warns them that God is angry but is dismissed with what is considered reasonable solutions. They continued to do evil things and speak in evil ways. So, God began to send their enemies against them in drones. Then finally, he turned them against themselves to consume each other in the midst of their lust.

## HOPEFUL, THANKFUL, BLESSED.

The day I was baptized as an adult I was high. It's true. I'd been living a life full of sin and it was struggling to keep me. But God.

As an addict, I made a ton of horrible choices. In the midst of my lowest moments, I turned to God for help. I began reading the Bible. I heard God's voice. But, I was teeter tottering with one foot in and one foot out.

I remember reading about false gods and God's jealousy. I started to drop off money at different churches. It wasn't necessarily a tithe, but it was an exact match to the amount I'd spent on drugs that week. So, whether that was $50 or $100, it was going to God. I wanted God to know, I didn't think the drug was bigger or more important than him in my life.

I tried to stop doing drugs. Several times. But, it kept calling me back. All it would take is a serious emotional hit that I didn't want to feel to make me desire the numbing effect.

One day, I am dropping off my money (I would just go when I thought church was over or when it was closed and slip it under the door) and this man named Mr. Smith walks out. He asks me, "If you die today would you know you are going to heaven?" Now I grew up in church and I have been baptized, so naturally, the textbook answer is yes. But my heart said no. So, I said no.

He then invited me to a class they give for people that want to know more about baptism and God. It was a couple of weeks. I am sure I arrived high for every class, but I was there. I was also studying the Bible because it simply intrigued me. My favorite books (still) were 1st and 2nd Kings. I loved to hear the amazing stories and God's sovereignty was evident.

So anyway, they set a date for baptism. Something happened and they had to change the date. I was in the middle of an off again on again season with the drugs. First date I was off, the second date they set (a month later) I was back on.

The night before I was to be baptized I had a lot going on in my mind. Was this real? Could I really commit to God? Isn't that what this meant? One of the guys that I would buy coke from was going to jail the next day. I'd gone over to his house to score and he invited me in to spend some time with he and his friends before he went to jail. I'd been talking to him about Jesus (as I did with all my dealers at the time -- ironic as it may be) and his love for us in spite of us.

While there, he pulled me to the side and he said, "Stephanie, it's time for you to go. We are about to start doing some heavy stuff and you don't need to be here. You need to go and get ready for tomorrow."

Now, I have to tell you how much this one moment means to me. It was a defining moment. You see, I hear so many people judge drug addicts and alcoholics and homeless people who have issues but I rarely hear of them truly helping them or just showering them with love. But some of the best GODLY advice I have ever received came from some of those folks because their relationships with God were intimate, sincere and real. This young man cared about me because I told him that God loved him right where he was. He looked out for me in a way many won't understand but I do. Drugs are serious strongholds. I remember feeling like I was in a personal prison I couldn't free myself from.

At any rate, the next day, I arrive at the church (family in tow) to get baptized. I was still high from partying the night before. When I walked down into that water, the minister looked at me intently. He hesitated. It was almost as if I could see God whispering in this man's ear that it was OK, because his disposition changed and he motioned for me to come forward and he dropped me down in the water.

My husband and children were so proud, but I was simply grateful. My change didn't happen overnight but it did come. What God taught me with my own life is that we have to extend love to those that get overlooked... that have been overlooked.

The best gift I ever received was a sincere relationship with Jesus

Christ and it was the brightest day.

*"Now when Jesus was risen early the first day of the week, he appeared first to Mary Magdalene, out of whom he had cast seven devils."*
*Mark 16:9*

## In Context
After the death and burial of Christ, Mary Magdalene, Salome and his mother went to anoint his body with oils and spices. As they wondered who would move the heavy stone in front of his tomb, they looked up and saw it had already been rolled away. They entered the tomb and was met by an angel who told them Christ would meet them where he promised. Stunned, afraid and full of amazement the ladies departed, speechless. As Mary Magdalene went her way, she was the first to see the Lord. She told the disciples but they didn't believe her until Jesus appeared before them as well. After, they went to preach the Gospel of Jesus Christ throughout the earth.

## Final Notes
The day Jesus was born, the day he was resurrected and the day he saved my life are the brightest moments I can share. I don't know about your journey. I don't know how you came to have a relationship with Christ or if you even have a relationship with Jesus. But if you do or when you do, I am certain it is also your brightest day.

### Prayer
Lord, I thank you that our testimony isn't pretty or glamorous. I thank you that you find yourself not bigger, grander, or so high-minded that you couldn't reach down and save a wretch like me. I thank you for your mercy and your grace. I thank you for your blessings. Lord, as we live the beautiful life you died to give please help us to reach others that are lost and hurting. Help us to become perfect conduits of your love. While we are not perfect or without sin, please forgive us when we fall short of your will. Thank you for your unending gift of presence and for the rivers of living water you are so willing to share.
*In Jesus Name, Amen.*

# The Darkest Hour

*"And Jesus answered them, saying, The hour is come, that the Son of man should be glorified. Verily, verily, I say unto you, Except a corn of wheat fall into the ground and die, it abideth alone: but if it die, it bringeth forth much fruit."*
*John 12:23-24*

## In Context

Jesus shares the untimely truth about what is to come and why it must happen. The chapter opens with Jesus and his disciples having dinner at Lazarus, Mary and Martha's house. Mary anoints Jesus' feet with an expensive ointment preparing him for burial. Many traveled to see Lazarus who'd been raised from the dead but by the next day many more came for the Passover and because they knew that Jesus would be there. Carrying palm leaves they shouted, "Hosanna, Blessed is the King of Israel that cometh in the Name of the Lord". Jesus rode through the town on the back of a donkey. The worship of Jesus made the Pharisees very nervous. A fellowship of Greeks traveled to meet and see Jesus. Jesus then informed his disciples of the impending trouble to come. He vowed the importance of what must happen and ended with "Father, Glorify thy name." To which God responded, "I have both glorified it and shall glorify it again." (I have to stop and wonder is God referring to the revelation of the Father, The Son and then the upcoming revelation of the Holy Ghost?) Jesus assured those surrounding him that God spoke for their benefit and reassured them again, why he must die in order to save others. Then Jesus responded, "Yet, a little while is the light with you. Walk while ye have the light, lest darkness come upon you: for the that walketh in darkness knoweth not where he goeth. While ye have the light believe in the light that you may be the children of light." Many refused to believe him, while others that did believe were afraid to say so (they loved what men thought of them more than what God thought of them). Finally, Jesus ended with an affirmation that any man that believed in him, believed also in God and saw God in him. That any man that did not see God in him, not only did not know God but could not see God because he was sent by God.

## KILLING THE LIFE I THOUGHT I LOVED

We walk with a sense of pride. Titles, associations, beauty, influence… they all make us desire more and more of them to become more powerful. I am no different than any other person walking this earth that desires those things – or at least at one time I did.

In my late twenties, I was beautiful. I had a great job with authority. I was popular. I lived in one of the most wonderful cities and made a great income. But, I let the power associated with all those things go to my head. Seeking more and more of it, my life began to crumble around me.

I could have and or get pretty much anything I wanted. My friends carried more power and were connected to more money than I could imagine and if I greatly desired it, I could get it.

This was a dangerous place to be in. I have always carried a little weight on me. My average body size was 9 – 11. Which in Atlanta is thick. I wanted to be thinner. I needed the weave, the manicures and pedicures, the nice car and nice apartment. I needed it all to live up to the image I felt I carried.

I began to do drugs. At first, it was recreational – just for fun. But I began to find the more I did, the more weight I dropped. I was down to a size 4 and I was beautiful (or so I thought).

My life was becoming ugly and dim. I was burning bridges with everyone I knew. I began to have anxiety attacks and went to get treated. What they prescribed was harder than the street drugs I chose to ingest! I broke down. I grabbed the Bible and said, "God if there is anything to this, you have to show me now." And he did.

But I had to lose it all. I lost my house (by then I'd put $7K down on my dream house), my husband (who'd reconnected with me by then), my friends (everyone that I had fun partying with) and was left with me. The me I didn't want to love. The me I didn't want to face. The unfiltered mirrored reflection that was me. That me had to let Jesus in because he'd been knocking on my door for far too long.

*"Now from the sixth hour there was darkness over all the land*
*unto the ninth hour."*
*Matthew 27:45*

## In Context

The crucifixion of Jesus Christ is detailed in Matthew 27. The chapter opens with a repentful Judas trying to make things right. When hope seems lost, he hangs himself. The elders who paid him, also feeling guilty bury their "blood" money in a field where strangers are buried. Then Jesus is delivered to Pontius Pilate. Pilate's wife has nightmares about their involvement and insists Pilate have nothing to do with it. Pilate knows this accusation is coming from a place of envy so he tries to make it right. He takes Jesus and a convicted murderer before the people to choose who should be crucified. The Pharisees and Sadducees incite the crowd to free the murderer. Pilate confirms and acknowledges that he has nothing to do with their choice. They insist and scream, "His blood be on us and our children." Soldiers take Jesus away and place him in a robe and mockingly place a crown of thorns on his head. Then they took him to Golgotha and crucified him on the cross. They gave him vinegar to drink. They gambled for his clothing. The elders, religious priests and people mocked him saying, "He trusted in God, let him deliver him now, if he will save him: for he said I am the Son of God." Then it became dark. After 3 hours, Jesus cried out to God. "God, my God, why hast thou forsaken me?" Jesus cried once more in anguish and died on the cross. It was the darkest moment. There was an earthquake. Graves opened up and saints that were dead arose and went to heaven. Later a rich follower of Jesus begged his body and provided a proper burial process, wrapping him in fine linen. Then they placed his body in a tomb that was sealed with a heavy stone and guarded by watchmen.

## Final Notes

In the darkest hour, there is new life. Sometimes death is required before new life can begin. Bad habits must die so good habits can bless. Old relationships must expire so new ones can begin. Death to anything invites new life.

---

### Prayer

Lord Jesus. Thank you. We don't know why or how you choose to move. We can only accept the path you have provided with grace and humility. Help us to embrace the abrupt changes you bring into our lives. Take our hands, whisper in our ears and assure us with your words of wisdom. We do not know what tomorrow will bring, we simply ask that you help us during the transition from this life into the next.

We love you, we give you glory, honor and praise.

*In Jesus Name, Amen.*

---

# Where is He?

*"When John the Baptist was in prison, he heard what Jesus was doing. He sent his followers. They asked, "Are You the One Who was to come, or should we look for another?" Jesus said to them, "Go and tell John what you see and hear. The blind are made to see. Those who could not walk are walking. Those who have had bad skin diseases are healed. Those who could not hear are hearing. The dead are raised up to life and the Good News is preached to poor people. He is happy who is not ashamed of Me and does not turn away because of Me."*
*Matthew 11:2-6*

## In Context

In Matthew 11, John the Baptist is imprisoned (and in later chapters, eventually beheaded). He is able to see his fate and is concerned he has been preaching on behalf of a farce. Why wouldn't the man he has told the world is so great save him from such a great downfall? He sends his disciples to question Jesus. Jesus responds by asking them to witness his miracles and report them. Then he tells the crowd how great and wonderful John actually is and that he is the one that has preached about for years to come. He notes that John is the greatest man to walk the earth that has not been born again (in the Spirit). Then Jesus begins to speak to the communities that refuse to change. He touts the miracles that have been done before them would have changed cities with worse reputations. Finally, he finishes where he began, stating that a man that is heavy with burdens (such as John) can find rest in him.

## TIRED, WORN OUT AND OVER IT.

I grew up in church. My mom was a Christian. My father was a Christian. My grandparents were Christian. I went to church every Sunday. I was one of the Sunday School secretaries. I sang in the choir. I was on the drill team. I went to every Baptist Convention possible. I participated in every Easter play, Christmas play and everything in between.

But I was still angry. I was molested at a young age. My parents were divorced and it ruined my life. I saw one of my friends die in front of me. I married young and it didn't end well. I was raped… and life as a single parent was horrific, lonely and overwhelming.

I was angry… at God. While many of my hardships came from poor personal decisions, he still got the blame. All I could think was, if God is real, "Where is he?" Why is he allowing all of this crap to happen and why does my life have to be so miserable?

I remember a day when my brother and sister came over after a tough week. I think I'd totaled my 3rd car in a year. They told me I need Jesus. I remember laughing at them. They didn't care. Now they wanted to tell me what I should do? I was angry.

But life only got tougher. Eventually, I found myself in front of that Bible telling God that if there was anything to this, I needed him to show me. I invited God into my life because it was a mess and I didn't know what to do except give up.

Not only did God show up, he showed out. I was free. Everything that bothered me seemed to get much better when I learned to hand each of those problems over to Jesus.

> *"And at midnight Paul and Silas prayed, and sang praises unto God: and the prisoners heard them. And suddenly there was a great earthquake, so that the foundations of the prison were shaken: and immediately all the doors were opened, and every one's bands were loosed."*
> *Acts 16 :25-26*

## In Context

Paul and Silas traveled the world to share the Gospel of Jesus Christ. After going as the Holy Spirit instructed, Paul had a dream to travel to Macedonia. There they met a woman who asked to be baptized with her family. Filled with the Spirit of God, she invited the men to come to her house to stay the evening. While at her house, another woman – a psychic of sorts, began to follow them and shout behind them that they were great prophets of God (trying to make her employers more money in the process). Paul became irritated and turned around as she followed. He commanded the evil spirit within in her to leave and it was gone out of the woman within the hour. Her employers became angry and accused Paul and Silas before the magistrate. This then caused both men to be beaten and thrown into jail. Late in the midnight hour, Paul and Silas began praising God and singing thanks. This caused an earthquake and all of the prison doors to open, allowing escape but none escaped. The guard of the prison was amazed and became a believer instantly. He begged Paul and Silas to come to his house to teach himself and his family. They obliged and the man's entire family was baptized that evening. The next day, the magistrate heard the story and asked Paul and Silas to leave because they were very afraid. They then returned to the woman of God's house for rest and comfort.

## Final Notes

Regardless of the outcome, God has a purpose for our lives. Every day will not be glamourous or great, but each is important. Many in the Bible suffered to further the Kingdom of God. Whether it was Moses (who wasn't permitted to go over into the Promised Land), or John the Baptist (who was beheaded and hung upside down on a cross) or Stephen (who was stoned to death while looking up into heaven as he was murdered), there were many who lived a life of service to God without external "glory". Jesus said many are blessed who are persecuted for the sake of God's kingdom. In the end, we can praise God regardless of outcome, understanding that we still win.

### Prayer

Most gracious and heavenly Father, thank you for your Word on today. We bless you and praise you in the Holy and Righteous name of Jesus. We thank you for paying the ultimate cost to save us from ourselves. Without your mercy and grace, where would we be? Lord, we ask that you direct our paths and make them straight. That you help us to humbly obey and know that in the midst of our worst circumstance, you are still on the throne. We know that you see and know what we need before we open our mouths to ask and for that we thank you.
We love you and praise your Holy Name.
*In Jesus Name, Amen.*

# Speak Lord, Your Servant is Listening

*"So then faith cometh by hearing, and hearing by the word of God."*
*Romans 10:17*

## In Context

The salvation presented by Jesus Christ is a blessing to receive. Romans 10 helps any person understand what salvation is and how it can be achieved. It further clarifies that it is not obtained by traditional religious acts or vain ramblings but by accepting Jesus as our Lord and openly admitting that we need him in our lives to survive. Then God will do the work. But, we have to be willing to let him in

## AN OPEN HEART, AN OPEN MIND AND LISTENING EARS

So many times since I have been saved I have heard God speak to me. However, I have never heard his voice more clearly than the moment I decided I was going to trust God to save me.

It was a morning not long after my 30th birthday. I'd been partying all night at a recording studio in Atlanta. I was depressed. Ironically, those two should never go hand-in-hand. My activities led to an evening of tears in a back room for more than 6 hours. It was very early in the morning and I decided, I can't do this here. I have to go home and get this sorted out in my heart.

I'd been reading the Bible for about 3 months at this point. I knew

God was teaching me from his word each day as I read because it always made me feel better and more connected to God.

Well, the journey from the recording studio to my home normally took about 40 minutes without traffic. As I got onto the highway, I thought 'no one loves me'. Suddenly on the radio, Whitney Houston's song, 'I will always love you' came on. While enjoying the song, I thought, 'What am I doing with my life'. Suddenly, as I passed a billboard on the highway, the message echoed my thought. I reflected, and whispered a small 'wow'. Then as I switched over to another highway, I thought about something at work. Then the DJ on the radio said, "Are you having issues with xxx at work?" XXX being exactly what I was thinking about and I was dumbfounded. I thought, 'OK, this is weird and it has to be God'.

It was in that moment that I had a real revelation that Jesus is real. That he knows everything I am thinking, every emotion I feel and every choice I am going to make. In a way it comforted me, but my first emotion was fear. I can't lie. Sometimes you just want to think your thoughts are private. LOL. But, nope, the good thing is that you aren't left alone to figure it out in this world. I was happy that there was someone I could trust with the things too horrible to say in words and too difficult to handle on my own.

*"Hear, O Lord, when I cry with my voice: have mercy also upon me, and answer me."*
*Psalm 27:7*

**In Context**
I won't fear my enemies because I can trust God. They are going to come and try to take my place but God has my back. All I have to do is believe and receive.

**Final Notes**
When you have a great relationship with God, you can have conversations with God. That means you can talk to Him AND listen. God knows exactly how to reach you. What you have to do is be ready to hear what he has to say because he is going to bless you.

The Israelites in the Bible understood worship in its most traditional sense. What they didn't grasp or refused to grasp was a sincere relationship with God. Don't get caught up in the show of religion without getting the point – to have a blessed, fruitful and peaceful life walking and talking with Jesus.

---

### Prayer
Lord, you really know us. Every part, good and bad. How wonderful it is to praise you, how marvelous it is to trust you. It is amazing to know that you care about and truly know about every intricate detail of each person living. As we walk this journey, make us boldly aware of your presence. Help us to expect, recognize, listen and embrace your message. Empower us with child-like trust, unapologetic obedience to your Word and a simple way to remember that you know, you care and you live.
*In Jesus Name, Amen.*

## DAY 29

# Lost & Confused, But OK

*"And he said unto him, If now I have found grace in thy sight, then shew me a sign that thou talkest with me."*
*Judges 7:17*

## In Context

Israel was in a tough place. After many victories, they found themselves back in sin and under the rule of the Midianites who stole everything they had. A young man named Gideon was hiding behind a wine-press threshing wheat when an angel of God approached him with a message. God told him that he would take down the Midianites as one man. Gideon couldn't help but be afraid. He didn't feel equipped. He didn't feel like he was able. He asked God for a sign to strengthen him.

## <u>An Open Heart, An Open Mind and Listening Ears</u>

So many times since I have been saved I have heard God speak to me. However, I have never heard his voice more clearly than the moment I decided I was going to trust God with my life.

It was a morning not long after my 30th birthday. I'd been partying all night at a recording studio in Atlanta. I was depressed. Ironically, those two should never go hand-in-hand. My activities led to an evening of tears in a back room for more than 6 hours. It was very early in the morning and I decided, I can't do this here. I have to go home and get this sorted out in my heart.

I'd been reading the Bible for about 3 months at this point. I knew God was teaching me from his word each day as I read because it always made me feel better and more connected to God.

Well, the journey from the recording studio to my home normally took about 40 minutes without traffic. As I got onto the highway, I thought 'no one loves me'. Suddenly on the radio, Whitney Houston's song, 'I will always love you' came on. While enjoying the song, I thought, 'What am I doing with my life'. Suddenly, as I passed a billboard on the highway, the message echoed my thought. I reflected, and whispered a small 'wow'. Then as I switched over to another highway, I thought about something at work. Then the DJ on the radio said, "Are you having issues with xxx at work?" XXX being exactly what I was thinking about and I was dumbfounded. I thought, 'OK, this is weird and it has to be God'.

It was in that moment that I had a real revelation that Jesus is real. That he knows everything I am thinking, every emotion I feel and every choice I am going to make. In a way it comforted me, but my first emotion was fear. I can't lie. Sometimes you just want to think your thoughts are private. LOL. But, nope, the good thing is that you aren't left alone to figure it out in this world. I was happy that there was someone I could trust with the things too horrible to say in words and too difficult to handle on my own.

*"For the Lord God will help me; therefore shall I not be confounded: therefore have I set my face like a flint, and I know that I shall not be ashamed."*
*Isaiah 50:7*

**In Context**
God is able to save me when we trust him. If we fan the flames of trouble, we will get what we are looking for. Isaiah 50 is about the sheer reverence of God. Not only trusting him, but trusting him in the face of adversity. It's also about being obedient to what God says we must do.

**Final Notes**
In order to win victory over the battles we face in life, we must not only recognize God's voice but we must also learn to obey his orders. Trying to solve our problems our way will have us up at

the midnight our crying our eyes out over situations we have NO POWER to change. When we release our situations to God and allow him to fight, we are showing we trust him, believe him and are willing to obey him. We will face situations that will be unfair and seem troublesome, but all we have to do is hold on to God's unchanging hand.

---

### Prayer

Most gracious and heavenly Father, we hear you knocking at the door of our hearts and we will not ignore you. Lord, instead we release our fight to you. We understand and know that we are not in a position to judge and that are only job is to obey you. Help us to be peaceable in the face of adversity, to be loving in the midst of pain, to be strong when we want to cry out in weakness and to clearly hear your words of encouragement and direction with a heart willing to obey.

*In Jesus Name, Amen.*

---

DAY
**30**

# In His Favor, There is Peace

*"Glory to God in the highest heaven, and on earth peace to those on whom his favor rests."*
*Luke 2:14*

## In Context

A man and his fiancée travel home for an important census. While there, his fiancée goes into labor. She was forced to deliver the baby in an outdoor stall for animals (due to so many coming into town for the census). Shepherds that were nearby were visited by an angel and told that The Messiah of the world had just been born. The angel told the shepherds to look for a baby wrapped in blankets lying in an animal stall. Suddenly, a host of angels began singing next to the angel with the message. The shepherds moved quickly to find the baby the angel spoke of. They began to share the message with everyone they met along the way. When they reached Mary, the mother of the baby, she was quiet but inwardly processing what the shepherds shared. 8 days later the baby was circumcised and named Jesus. Afterward, an older man named Simeon met Jesus. He'd waited his entire life to meet him as he prayed to God to allow him to live to meet the Messiah. As he prophesied over the child another prophet named Anna began to prophesy.

Twelve years later, the man and his now wife brought Jesus to

Jerusalem (as they did every year) for the Feast of Passover. When it was time to go home, the family traveled the long trek, only to discover Jesus was not with them. They panicked, returned to Jerusalem to find him in the church with the elders, asking questions and having a great dialogue. The elders were impressed with his knowledge but his parents were wrought. Jesus responded, "Where else would I be? I am about my father's business," he stated, referring to God.

## WHICH WAY IS UP?

I have always loved that movie by Richard Pryor. The story is of a man who finds love and success after a hard life of struggle. After basking in his new found success for a short while he begins to feel "privileged" and begins to treat those who helped him and love his as servants and meaningless accessories to his life.

I remember a time when I helped someone by doing everything I could to help them be successful and soon the very same thing occurred. No matter how much or how great, it was never enough. They wanted more and more and more. While my role was diminished or treated as if I was unimportant. It angered me. I felt used, overlooked, bitter, and out of control.

Inside I knew that the person I helped wasn't my assignment, it was God's assignment. But I was still experiencing a great amount of pain. To every assignment, there is a season. So, just as a great and mighty wind of change will bring you into someone's life, there is a time when another wind will bring you out... if that is what God desires. We have to be willing to accept God's desire over our own.

In life, we experience pain. It's a fact. How we manage that pain is where we often fail and fall. In God's Favor, there is peace. Peace allows you to accept God's will in the midst of pain and trust that he is bringing you into a new season of reaping or sowing. Either way, it will be good for you.

*"Anyone who claims to live in God's light and hates a brother or sister is still in the dark. It's the person who loves brother and sister who dwells in God's light*

*and doesn't block the light from others. But whoever hates is still in the dark,*
*stumbles around in the dark, doesn't know which end is up, blinded by the*
*darkness."*
I John 2: 9-11, MSG

## In Context
I John 2 is a guide to understanding sin and how to walk in Christ. It begins by describing how to recognize whether you are living in sin. Next it warns of the way of the world, the antichrist and deception. Finally, it strongly encourages you to live in Christ.

## Final Notes
In God's Favor, we have abundant peace. No matter the situation or outcome, we can rest knowing God has our back. He is working everything out for our good. His plan for our lives is intricate and full of interesting twists and turns. Our job is to resist the fight that tries to tell us we are right and he is wrong. Go with the flow and experience God's favor and God's peace in any situation... No matter how difficult it is, it isn't bigger than our God.

---

### Prayer
Lord Jesus, please help us to recognize which way is up. Help us not to get tangled in emotion. Help us to endure the pain while holding on to your promises of peace, provision and protection. Guide our every footstep. Help us harness our words and our actions as we move forward flowing with your wind of change. Lord, forgive us of our sins and help us forgive others as we seek to be more like you each day. Thank you for your love, your mercy and your grace. Thank you for the power of the Holy Spirit, who is our comforter and greatest friend.
*In Jesus Name, Amen.*

---

# Sovereign God

*"The grace of the Lord Jesus Christ, and the love of God, and the communion of the Holy Ghost, be with you all. Amen."*
*2 Corinthians 13:14*

## In Context

Paul wrote several letters to Corinth begging them to get right before God before his arrival in town. He knew and recognized his own limitations but also wanted them to be right before God. He spoke of his weakness and even the weakness Jesus reflected as he hung from the cross. In contrast, he spoke of the POWER of Christ in his ability to rise and reign over his kingdom with a sober mind, fairly dividing right from wrong. Along the same lines, he warned that when he arrived in Corinth, the same POWER of Christ would work through him to convict (not condemn) them into looking clearly at their situations. He also stated that if at investigation, error was found in his teaching, he would rather it be the case than knowing the people were choosing to sin outright and without concern for the kingdom of God. Finally, he advised them to love one another. He told them to be friendly, happy and agreeable trusting that the sovereignty of God would bless their lives.

## LOOKING GLASS

There are days when I truly hate to look in the mirror. Some days I look amazing and it sparks my day. Others, I am not up to par and I am trying to figure out what I need to do in order to reflect the image I desire.

One day, as I was disgusted, looking at myself in the mirror, I realized I wasn't seeing my physical reflection… I was looking at my soul. The core of my being… and I didn't like it at all. I'd been making decisions that were selfish and I knew I hurt the people around me to get my way. I looked at the woman looking back at me and she was just ugly. Her attitude, her disposition, her thoughts… she needed a serious makeover and quickly.

I began to cry… uncontrollably. The choices I'd made in my selfishness were going to end in destruction I thought. I'd created so many little gods that were more important than Jesus: work, love, money, power, image… So many walls were closing in that I contemplated running away or suicide. I didn't know what to do.

That's when I felt a strong urge to pray.

I began to pray for God to give me a clean heart and a clean spirit. I begged God to forgive me and to help me be who he created me to be… not this person or image I was chasing to have others accept me. I instantly felt a strong wave of peace come over me.

When I got up off of my bathroom floor, I looked into the mirror and sure enough, the image I loved was back. I felt beautiful and confident that God's grace was all I needed to get through the season ahead. I knew that he was with me: protecting, guiding and being God over my life.

*"For thus saith the Lord God, the Holy One of Israel; In returning and rest shall ye be saved; in quietness and in confidence shall be your strength: and ye would not."*
*Isaiah 30:15*

## In Context

Isaiah 30 shares nothing but truth and it is the hard, realistic truth. Isaiah shares how God's people have the opportunity to have it all: blessings, peace and a quiet confidence knowing that God is sovereign… but they are choosing power, money, sex and evil instead. Isaiah also shares that God will not be disrespected in the end. He is sovereign and his way is the only way that will last. So, in the end, we have to stop trying to save ourselves (which is what causes us to sin) and have enough faith in God to allow him to do the work. Otherwise, we are bound to face a defeated life of hope in things that will never truly come to pass (it may seem to others as though we have arrived but it will be a life filled with misery, self-hate and defeat).

## Final Notes

God knows. God understands. God cares. He is sovereign. This means he has supreme, absolute, unlimited, unrestricted, boundless, ultimate, total and unconditional power over any and every situation we face. We can feel confident and safe turning our lives over to him in care because he loves us immensely. He has provided his Son as a constant reminder that he is willing to sacrifice his all for us, his Holy Spirit as comforter to get us through each day and himself as a Sovereign God, fairly ruling over it all.

---

### Prayer

Most gracious and heavenly father, we come before you with a humble heart filled with gratitude for your mercy, love and grace. We thank you for the perfect gift of salvation. Remove anything that isn't like you, please forgive us of our sins and help us to trust you with our lives. Help us to know and understand that your love is unending, your grace abounding and your mercies are new each morning. Help us to look in the mirror of our lives and love what we see, knowing we have allowed YOU to reign over our thoughts, hearts and spirits. Decrease our desires for more and increase our yearning for you. Help us to see clearly the direction we have chosen for our lives. If our compass needs adjusting, Lord, do what you must. We love you and thank you for our lives,
*In the matchless and holy name of Jesus we pray, Amen.*

---

# in HIS favor

**There is no fear where love exists.**
Rather, perfect love banishes fear, for fear involves punishment,
and the person who lives in fear has not been perfected in love.
*1 John 4:18*

**Do not be anxious about anything,**
but in everything by prayer and supplication with thanksgiving
let your requests be made known to God.
*Philippians 4:6*

**"Come to me, all who labor and are heavy laden,**
and I will give you rest. Take my yoke upon you, and learn from
me, for I am gentle and lowly in heart, and you will find rest for
your souls. For my yoke is easy, and my burden is light."
*Matthew 11:28-30*

**Peace I leave with you,**
my peace I give unto you: not as the world giveth, give I unto you.
Let not your heart be troubled, neither let it be afraid.
*John 14:27*

**He heals the brokenhearted**
and binds up their wounds.
*Psalm 147:3*

FAVOR

**F**

*Faith*

## WALKING IN THE RECOGNITION OF YOUR FAVOR REQUIRES FAITH.

*Speak, for your servant is listening.*
*I Samuel 3:10*

Reading the Bible, thanking God and prayer allow us to learn more about the Lord. These actions place us in a position to download into our hearts and minds the true essence of God's character. They allow us to not only believe in Him, but it also opens us to receive his Word, his love and his direction for our lives.

FAVOR
**A**

# *Action & Accountability*

WALKING IN THE RECOGNITION OF YOUR **FAVOR** REQUIRES
ACTION AND ACCOUNTABILITY.

*What good is it, my brothers, if someone says he has faith but does not have
works? Can that faith save him?*
James 2:14

A person prepared to walk in God's favor must take action. If we simply hear what God says and don't begin to take the actions required to see it come to pass, we are only fooling ourselves. Our confessed faith in God's promises require that our hands, feet and mouth agree.

**FAVOR**

**V**

# Virtuous Intimacy

Walking in the recognition of your **FAVOR** requires
virtuous intimacy.

*Create in me a clean heart, O God, and renew a right spirit within me.*
*Psalm 51:10*

In order to recognize the blessing that comes from worship, faith
and action, we must live righteously. Will God's favor rest on us
if we don't? Yes. He is no respecter of persons and he rains on
the just and the unjust (which is exemplified in my life story).
However, in order to walk in true recognition of his favor, we must
commune with him as much as possible. God knows the status of
our heart and our motives, so we must ask for his mercy which is
provided brand new each morning as we come to him in prayer. If
we are faithful to confess our sins and ask for forgiveness, God will
not only commune with us, he will reveal things that
we could not know.

# Obedience

**WALKING IN THE RECOGNITION OF YOUR FAVOR REQUIRES
OBEDIENCE.**

*Has the Lord as great delight in burnt offerings and sacrifices,
as in obeying the voice of the Lord? Behold, to obey is better than sacrifice,
and to listen than the fat of rams.*
1 Samuel 15: 22

Obedience is not easy. In fact, it is much easier for us to donate a
little more money or time than to follow the explicit instruction
of God. Why? Much like Jesus in his final moments, crying for his
father to take the cup of obedience from him, we too must have
a "never the less" spirit... and that isn't always the most enjoyable
route. Sometimes God asks us to forgive and serve those that have
hurt us. Sometimes God asks us to give up something we have
desired our entire lives and possibly just been given to do his will
above our own. Sometimes we are asked to sacrifice someone we
love for God's purpose. It isn't easy to obey, but when you do, you
will recognize that God will give you the desires of your heart,
which will also be more than you can ask, think or imagine. You
will taste and see that the Lord is indeed, good.

FAVOR

**R**

*Rest*

## WALKING IN THE RECOGNITION OF YOUR FAVOR REQUIRES REST.

*There is nothing better for a person than that he should eat and drink and find enjoyment in his toil. This also, I saw, is from the hand of God, for apart from him who can eat or who can have enjoyment?*
*Ecclesiastes 2:24-25*

The power of rest allows for reflection, rejuvenation, response and recognition. Rest is required in order to prepare for the next leg of the journey and the next battle of the war. In God's favor we are on a battlefield, but we know that victory is ours. This is how and why we are able to rest. This is also why God has established a specific time of resting and it is a mandate he expects us to obey. Resting allows you to recognize the favor God has placed on your life and know, that God is good and that you are "In HIS Favor".

# FAVOR

Faith.
Action & Accountability.
Virtuous Intimacy.
Obedience.
Rest.

My prayer is that this devotional has blessed you. I have no idea what God has in store for your tomorrows, but I pray that with the help of this devotional, you have the ability to recognize and understand that you are forever resting in HIS favor as the apple of his eye. I know from personal experience that God never delights in the bad things that may happen to us. He allows some things to occur in order to mature us to a level of understanding and knowledge that even in bad times, he is still sovereign and good.

I love you and I am praying for your strength, perseverance, abundance and love.

May God Bless You and Keep You,

*Stephanie Moore*

www.ingramcontent.com/pod-product-compliance
Lightning Source LLC
Chambersburg PA
CBHW061728020426
42331CB00006B/1144